RAILROAD COLOR HISTORY

UNION PACIFIC
RAILROAD

BRIAN SOLOMON

Voyageur Press

First published in 2000 by Voyageur Press, an imprint of MBI Publishing Company, Galtier Plaza, Suite 200, 380 Jackson Street, St. Paul, MN 55101 USA.

Library of Congress Cataloging-in-Publication Data Available

ISBN 13: 978-0-7603-0756-4
ISBN 10: 0-7603-0756-3

Book design and layout by Mike Schafer and Maureene D. Gulbrandsen/Andover Junction Publications, Blairstown, New Jersey, and Lee, Illinois.

Edited by Mike Schafer/Andover Junction Publications
Cover design by Tom Heffron

Printed in China

Front cover: Four Union Pacific locomotives grind their way over California's Altamont Pass on the old Western Pacific main line on the morning of February 23, 1990, with an eastbound freight out of the San Francisco Bay area. *Brian Solomon*

Frontispiece: Union Pacific's long-lived shield has become one of the most-recognized emblems in American transporation. *Ron Lundstrom*

Title page: An eastbound Union Pacific freight flying along at North Polodor, Wyoming, appears to be attempting to outrun approaching thunderstorms on October 3, 1993. *Don Marson*

Verso page: A Union Pacific caboose at Antioch, California, in 1992 sports one of UP's many slogans. *Brian Solomon*

Acknowledgments page: In 1969, one of Union Pacific's behemoth 8,500-hp. General Electri gas-turbine-electrics appears to be peering into the roundhouse at Cheyenne, Wyoming. *Mike Schafer*

Introduction page: Scenery and the UP are synonymous, as dramatically illustrated by an eastbound merchandise train at Palisade, Nevada, in September 1991. *George Pitarys*

Back cover top: UP's fleet of streamliners represented the best in American rail passenger service from the 1930s to the 1970s. Among its many "City" trains was the Domeliner *City of Denver*, shown at its namesake city in the spring of 1967. *Ron Lundstrom*

Back cover bottom: Say "Union Pacific" and many people immediately conjure up images of mammoth steam locomotives—and rightfully so. UP operated some of the largest locomotives in the world. In September 1957, one of the railroad's famous "Challenger"-type 4-6-6-4 steam engines rides the turntable at Cheyenne, Wyoming. *John Dziobko*

Contents

THE OVERLAND ROUTE

Acknowledgments

My experience with the Union Pacific spans just a little more than a decade, but in that time I've watched the railroad grow and transform itself into one of the largest transportation companies in the world.

My first encounter with the UP was an especially memorable one. I was on my way west and, following the advice of my longtime friend Robert A. Buck, was driving U.S. 30 across Nebraska. A day earlier I had been alerted to a special freight move using 4-8-4 No. 844 and had the fortuitous experience to follow the locomotive from Fremont, Nebraska, to Cheyenne, Wyoming, during a two-day span. What better way to see the Union Pacific for the first time!

Since that time I have observed Union Pacific operations all across its vast system, from northern Idaho to Louisiana, and from Southern California to Chicago, photographing it in all kinds of weather and from a variety of angles. On these numerous excursions I've been accompanied by several informed individuals who made the trips more enjoyable and rewarding. I would like to thank Tom S. Hoover, Brian L. Jennison, Mel Patrick, John Gruber, Blair Kooistra, Gerald Hook, Tom Danneman, Mike Danneman, Joe McMillan, and my father, Richard J. Solomon, among many others, for their company and insight .

In researching this book I consulted more than 50 books, dozens of periodicals, and sifted through piles of railroad literature. My father was especially generous with his library as was Bill Kratville and the Union Pacific Museum Collection. Mike Gardner and Brian L. Jennison also provided me with valuable materials and advice. Many people advised me on photo locations including J. D. Schmid, Brian Rutherford, Fred Matthews, and Mark Hemphill. I also would like to thank the many photographers that contributed to this project, as credited with their photos. Lori Swingle and Jennifer Thom of the Denver Public Library helped locate historical images. Tim Doherty was generous with his collection of vintage black & white images. Carl Swanson provided me with numerous amusing anedotes and stories involving his experiences with the UP and its enthusiasts and proponents. We also shared a memorable ride on a UP excusion over the former C&NW in the summer of 1995. Mike Shafer, Maureene Gulbrandsen, Jim Popson, Steve Smedley, and Steve Esposito of Andover Junction Publications were invaluable in their photo selection, production, and layout of the book. Lastly, I would like to thank all the employees of the Union Pacific who have worked to make it a better railroad.

—*Brian Solomon, 1999*

Introduction

Union Pacific's main line across Nebraska symbolizes the American high-density rail-freight business. This busy railroad raceway is saturated with traffic. Huge trains, often stretching out two miles long, roll along in ever-greater numbers. UP hauls everything from new automobiles to timber, grain, and coal.

UP's pioneering roll in Western development, its strategic centralized location, and low-grade profile has assured the railroad a healthy share of freight traffic. It was the first transcontinental route, and has long served as the nation's premier route to the coast. As the nation's economy has swelled, Union Pacific's freight traffic has grown, and today it is one of the busiest freight railroads in America. Its main line from Omaha across Nebraska and through Wyoming is a central conduit for east-west freight traffic.

In recent years UP's already busy east-west main line was made even busier when its longtime affiliate, Chicago & North Western, tapped into the lucrative Powder River coal traffic. North Western funneled the coal to UP rather than rebuild its own decrepit route across Nebraska, and now numerous heavy coal trains enter UP's Overland Route main line at O'Fallons, a few miles west of North Platte. By the mid-1990s, the combination of growing coal traffic, a robust economy, and UP's acquisition of C&NW and later Southern Pacific

has led the railroad to expand its capacity across Nebraska by building 108 miles of third main track between North Platte and Gibbon (where UP's line to Kansas City diverges) to augment its saturated double-track line. This $327 million project was completed in August 1999, and UP reports that as many as 140 freights roll between O'Fallons and Gibbon at the dawn of the new millennium.

Traditional Union Pacific routes have been melded with a host of other lines over the past two decades, and now the UP includes routes once operated by the Missouri Pacific, Western Pacific, Katy, Chicago & North Western, Southern Pacific, and portions of the old Rock Island. UP routes were once relatively straightforward; now they are complex, involving a myriad of track from Chicago to Los Angeles, and from New Orleans to Seattle. Union Pacific's famous shield is now as a familiar sight on Sherman Hill as it is in the California Sierra, the Louisiana bayou, or the New Mexico desert.

Now, Union Pacific is one of the largest railroads in the world. It operates 33,705 miles of railroad in 23 states, employs more than 33,000 people, owns nearly 7,000 diesel-electric locomotives, and more than 155,308 freight cars. Its vast, complex operations and long corporate history are intergral with America's growth and development.

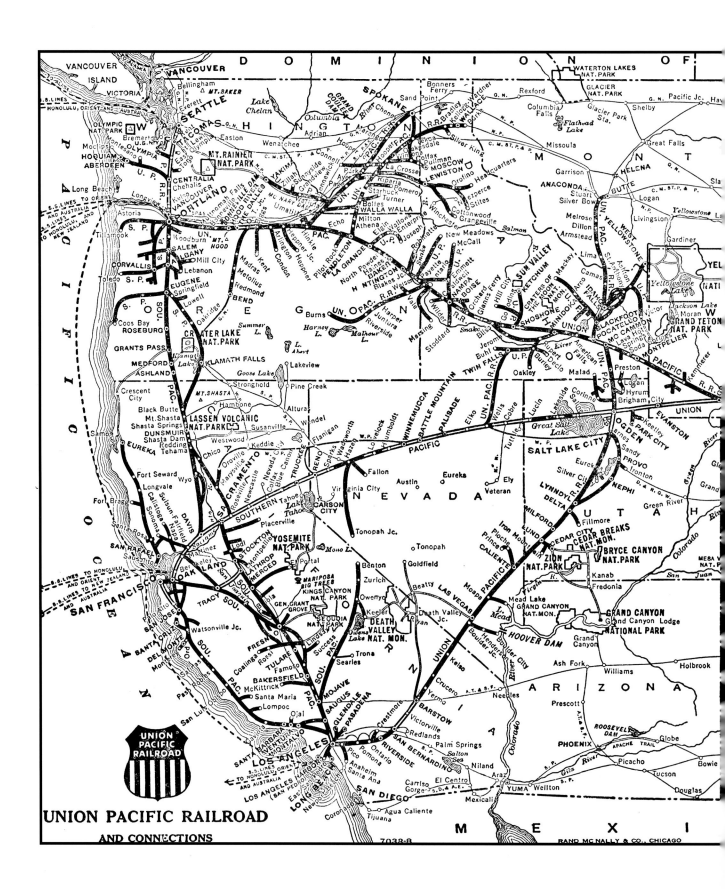

UNION PACIFIC RAILROAD

AND CONNECTIONS

8

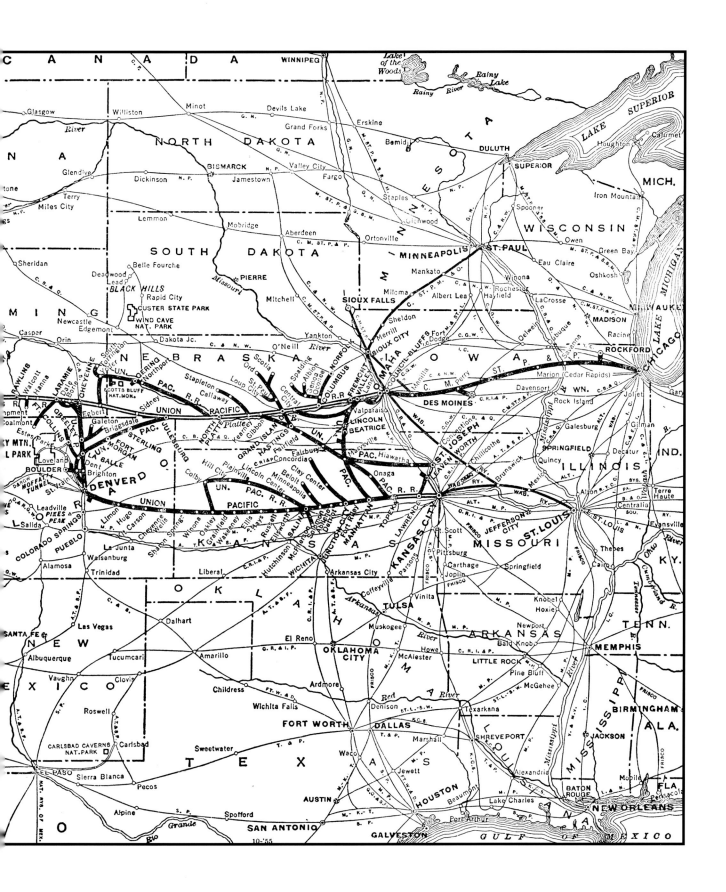

9

For all of the twentieth century, the Union Pacific Railroad has been an institution in American transportation. Known for its imposing steam locomotives (two of which were still operable as the new millennium dawned), Armour yellow diesels, and its instantly recognizable shield emblem, the Union Pacific has been an integral part of U.S. history since the 1860s. The UP's pride is reflected in this nose-on view of the railroad's business train at St. Louis in 1995. *Mike Schafer*

Westward Ho!

AMERICA HEADS "OVER THE LAND" TOWARD CALIFORNIA

Union Pacific is one of the oldest names in American railroading. Few companies—railroads or otherwise—have survived as long as the Union Pacific. The transcontinental railroad concept—which evolved into the Union Pacific—predates the railroad itself by three decades, and when it was finally built, the transcontinental railroad represented not just another rail line, but a fulfillment of national destiny. The UP was built as the eastern leg of the Pacific Railroad, that grandly inspired endeavor designed to span the vast wilderness known as the Great American Desert connecting east and west.

The first American railways dated to the late 1820s, when American entrepreneurs both imported and emulated British technology to build primitive lines in the eastern part of the nation. The Baltimore & Ohio was among the very first American railways. It was designed to reach the interior of the nation by connecting the port of Baltimore with the Ohio River. The railroad inspired development and facilitated settlement and growth. In the this formative time, forward-thinking visionaries conceived of a railway spanning the whole of America and reaching clear to the Pacific Coast. To most people, such a proposition seemed completely absurd. It was simply preposterous to think of a railroad crossing the mountain ranges and mysterious deserts that comprised the American West. The cost of such a project would be enormous, and there was no precedent for such a vast undertaking. In the 1830s most railroads were comparatively short affairs, rarely extending for more than a couple hundred miles and typically connecting a multitude of established population centers. It took decades for the transcontinental railroad concept to settle into the American consciousness.

By the 1840s the talk of a Pacific Railroad became more serious, and by the 1850s it had developed into a political issue. By then it was no longer just a matter of whether a transcontinental line would be built, but merely a matter of on which route and on what schedule. A handful of visionary engineers invested their own time and resources searching for the best routes well before money had been found to fund the construction of a Pacific Railroad. In California, Theodore Judah spent months in the Sierra surveying a route over the mountains, then played politics to drum up interest in his project. While most people dismissed Judah as "crazy," his ideas and surveys were well-founded and ultimately succeeded in securing both political support and financing for what became the Central Pacific.

While Judah was working in California, railroad builders and surveyors in the Middle West were eyeing the West as their next bold adventure. Railroads had pushed their way passed Chicago, onto the prairies of Illinois, across the mighty Mississippi, and were reaching farther afoot.

The motives for building westward were mixed. Some railway promoters were obviously just interested in lining their own pockets with quick profits from construction schemes; others saw the long-term potential of a transcontinental railroad. One of these forward thinkers was Grenville Dodge, who in the years preceding the Civil War made preliminary surveys west of the Missouri River. He became one of the foremost proponents of the Pacific Railway and had considerable influence in its ultimate construction. He was living near Council Bluffs, Iowa, in 1859 when he had a prophetic meeting with a certain presidential candidate by the name of Abraham Lincoln. Lincoln was campaigning and made a speech that made Dodge pause with interest. Lincoln was no stranger to the railroad, having worked as a lawyer for the Illinois Central, and he was very interested in the prospect of a transcontinental line. He met with Dodge in order to hear the engineer's theories on the subject. It is known that Lincoln wanted to learn what the best route west was, and interestingly it seems that Lincoln owned property at Council Bluffs, which seemed to be one of the choice locations of a railway terminal. Clearly both men were impressed with one another. Lincoln took Dodge's advice seriously while Dodge joined Lincoln's fledgling Republican Party and supported him in his presidential campaign. While no tracks would serve Council Bluffs for another six years, it would ultimately become the principle terminal and major junction for the proposed Pacific Railroad.

Lincoln was elected in 1860 and faced the greatest crisis that would afflict the United States—the American Civil War. The Pacific Railroad was finally born during the height of the strife between North and South. It was considered a strategic article during the war and designed in part to assure Union control of Western states.

In the years prior to the outbreak of the Civil War, a variety of general Pacific Railroad routes had been considered in Congress. Southern interests favored a more southerly route, located between the 32nd and 35th parallels, while Northern concerns obviously favored a more northerly path, ranging from a central route along the 41st and 42nd parallel, to a line much farther north. With the outbreak of the war, the central route won out and the names of the companies formed to build the railroad clearly reflected political nature of the project: Union Pacific and Central Pacific.

Interested parties lobbied Lincoln and Congress during the early 1860s and pushed their railroad proposals as a matter of strategic national importance. Some people felt that the government should simply build the railroad, while others were looking for governmental support of privately held firms. In both situations the chief impediment to the construction of the railroad was the exceptional costs involved. The Pacific Railroad represented the largest engineering project ever considered, and it faced several serious financial hurdles to overcome before it could be built. Unlike most American railways, the Pacific Railroad would be building through largely territory uninhabited, unsettled, and undeveloped by Europeans.

This had several serious implications, the first of which was a lack of supporting infrastructure. Basic tools, supplies, and labor would have to be imported hundreds of miles for use on the railway, dramatically increasing basic construction costs. Since the railroad would not immediately connect major population centers, it did not have good prospects for local traffic, as a result it would not be in a position to earn money until it was nearly completed. Another problem was local opposition. Just because European settlers were not living on the plains didn't mean this territory was uninhabited. In fact, several tribes of Native Americans had been living there quite contentedly for many generations. For the most part they were far less than pleased with the gradual encroachment of European civilization, and many people on both sides of the issue would die before it was "resolved." All of these concerns, combined with the enormous distances involved, discouraged investors and supporters within the government.

PACIFIC RAIL ACT OF 1862

To encourage investment and get the railroad moving, governmental support was necessary. Lincoln knew this, and on July 2, 1862, he signed the Pacific Rail Act authorizing the construction and funding of the project. While this act fueled interest in the transcontinental line and got both the Union Pacific and Central Pacific railroads going, it failed to generate significant finances to actually build the line. As a result, the Pacific Railroad made little progress despite initial government support. When it finally got going, the Pacific was fueled by patriotism, adventure . . . and greed. A year after the Pacific Rail Act was signed, the Union Pacific Railroad came to life. It was formed in

In a painting by noted railroad-theme artist Howard Fogg, the Missouri River separating Council Bluffs, Iowa, and Omaha, Nebraska, was still a barrier between east-west railroad transport in 1872, with freight and passengers having to be ferried across its waters. However, construction of UP's first bridge across the river is well under way. *Union Pacific Railroad Museum Collection*

A westbound UP freight out of Council Bluffs behind a trio of General Electric's massive U50-series locomotives exits the newer Missouri River bridge into Omaha on a summer morning in 1965. The bridge was also used by Burlington, Rock Island, Milwaukee Road, Chicago Great Western, and Wabash. *Ron Lundstrom*

Omaha was served by eight major railroads until the late 1960s, but it has always been very much a Union Pacific city. Although much of the railroad's terminal facilities are across the river in Council Bluffs, its headquarters is in Omaha proper. In this 1947 photo that looks northwesterly, Union Station stands bright and prominent in the lower left center. Farther to the left on the opposite side of the tracks is the Burlington Station. UP used Union Station, which opened its doors in 1931. Both depots remain standing in 2000. *Union Pacific Railroad Collection, image No. 77012*

October 1863 by a group of men that had worked together on a line building across Iowa.

THE UNION PACIFIC IS BORN

The leader and mastermind behind the Union Pacific was the notorious Thomas Durant—man who, according to John Hoyt Williams, author of *A Great and Shining Road*, would come to be the symbol of business corruption in America. Durant's physical appearance typified the villain in Vaudeville productions and early cinema. He wore a unkempt goatee, slicked-down hair, and dark suits. His dark, piercing eyes and cool expression gave him the look of a calculating, manipulative character.

Durant was born in the Berkshire Hills of western Massachusetts at the town of Lee in 1820 just a few years before railroad consciousness would sweep the nation. He studied medicine at Albany College and operated a private practice for a short time which earned him the nickname of "Doctor Durant," for which he is best remembered. In the 1850s he

worked for the Chicago & Rock Island, then later the Missouri & Mississippi, two prairie lines working their way westward. While working on these lines, Durant met a number of principal players in the early years of the Union Pacific including Grenville Dodge, John Dix, and Peter Dey. Even in his early railroading days, Durant was less interested in lofty aspirations of societal betterment, creating needed infrastructure, or the simple building of an adequate railway line than he was in lining his own pockets as quickly and quietly as he possibly could. He transferred these skills to the Union Pacific where his actions became legendary.

Durant served as vice president of the UP in its formative years while John A. Dix served as the line's first president. Despite the appearance of his secondary role, Durant, not Dix, was really in charge of the railroad. John Dix was a veteran of the War of 1812 who had served in a variety of prestigious positions, including as U. S. senator from New York and as U. S. Secretary of the Treasury. He had been

UP train 5, the daily Omaha–Los Angeles local, strolls out of Union Station on an August morning in 1967. Primarily a mail-and-express run, No. 5 was a connection for Milwaukee Road's overnight *Arrow* out of Chicago. *Mike Schafer*

UP diesels idle away the night hours at the Council Bluffs engine terminal in 1993. *David P. Oroszi*

president of the Missouri & Mississippi and was well-connected in Washington circles, qualities that made him especially useful to Durant.

Durant hired Peter Dey as Union Pacific's engineer. Dey was slightly younger than Durant. He was an honest, high-minded man of principle who had become a lawyer before studying engineering. He worked with Grenville Dodge to locate the best route west for the Union Pacific in the Platte River Valley. Despite his heartfelt desire to build the line, Dey's career with the UP was very short. His downfall was that he saw through Doctor

Durant's corrupt machinations and was tormented by them. In protest, he resigned his prestigious position as chief engineer. Grenville Dodge was quickly promoted in his place. Dodge was an equally good engineer and politically more powerful than Dey. While he worked with Durant to overcome a variety of problems, he stood his ground on several occasions when Durant's overt greed threatened to undermine the viability of the railroad.

OMAHA OR COUNCIL BLUFFS?

Although he was later condemned, Durant's sly, self-serving motives and backhanded approach to business got the Union Pacific moving. He established company offices in New York City, helped create the railroad construction company called the Credit Mobilier, and lobbied President Lincoln to establish Omaha as the railroad's eastern terminus. The Pacific Rail Act of 1862 had failed to establish a starting point, making it difficult for the eastern segment of the transcontinental line to get moving. There were several choices for an eastern terminus and considerable discussion as to where it should be. Omaha and Council Bluffs, which sat opposite one another on the Missouri River, had been two leading candidates.

From today's perspective, either Omaha Council Bluffs may seem like odd places to begin a transcontinental line, especially considering that they are nearly halfway across the country and were not yet served by a railway line. In fact, the nearest railroad in 1863 was many miles east of Council Bluffs. Essentially Omaha was a remote outpost on the edge of the frontier. So what was the attraction?

These towns sat at the eastern end of the Platte River Valley, the broad natural corridor to the west that Dodge, Dey, and others had long felt was obviously the best route for the railroad to build westward across the plains. Omaha/Council Bluffs were accessible by boats

traversing the Missouri, and although they were not yet served by a direct rail route, it was assumed that a railroad would soon be built to the Missouri River from the east. As it turned out, Lincoln and others were a bit optimistic in this regard. Tracks finally reached Council Bluffs in the mid-1860s, but the Missouri River was not bridged to Omaha until 1872, nearly a decade after it had been designated as the original eastern terminal. In 1864 the official terminal had been moved across the river to Council Bluffs.

DURANT SECURES A BETTER DEAL

The Union Pacific staged a gala public display in November 1863 at Omaha where the governor of Nebraska moved a shovelful of earth, brass bands played, and fireworks exploded in the sky. While enthusiasm for the railroad was high, funding was virtually non-existent. The initial Pacific Rail Act had fallen flat, and both Union Pacific and Central Pacific were starved for funds needed to build the railroad. So, despite this public display, the railroad remained a long way from the Pacific, and the Nebraska governor would need to shovel a lot more earth before the tracks were ready for the first locomotive!

Durant was well aware of this, so he and Central Pacific's Collis P. Huntington lobbied Lincoln to amend the 1862 Pacific Railroad Act for terms that were likely to attract serious investment. Lincoln complied, and the 1864 revisions put both companies in a better financial position to connect the nation. With the revised act, government bonds would be issued to the railroad for every 20 miles of track completed, allowing the railroad to generate money as the railroad was built. The bonds would eventually have to be paid back, but in the short term this provided cash for construction. The land-grant provision of the act was more liberal, giving Union Pacific roughly 12,000 acres per completed mile of track—approximately double that authorized by the Pacific Railroad Act of 1862. Furthermore, the land would include mineral rights, making it significantly more valuable to the railroad and potential investors.

CREDIT MOBILIER

Union Pacific's construction company, Credit Mobilier, which borrowed its name from a similar French concern, resembled typical railroad construction firms of the period. At this time it was not unusual for railroads to pay their own construction company to

One of the most famous locations on the original UP Overland Route main line is Sherman Hill, here being surmounted by an eastbound freight led by "Centennial" No. 6945 on an August morning in 1979. At 8,015 feet, Sherman is the highest point on the first transcontinental main line—but it is *not* the crossing of the Continental Divide, which is some 170 miles west of Sherman. *Steve Smedley* build the line. However, Credit Mobilier stretched the concept to new limits. Credit Mobilier made handsome profits by extracting as much money from the government in the form of land grants and bonds as it could while cutting corners on construction. Durant played a shrewd game to ensure maximum profits from railroad building. He inflated cost estimates for construction, in some cases nearly doubling what his engineers thought it would actually cost to build the railroad. Thus the dividends paid by the Credit Mobilier earned from construction of the Union Pacific made its owners very rich at the expense of the railroad and the taxpayer. What was especially devious about this arrangement was that the owners of Credit Mobilier were largely the very same men who controlled the UP. Furthermore, a number of them also held influential political positions and plied gifts of Credit Mobilier stock for personal and political gain.

In 1873, several years after the completion of the transcontinental railroad, the excesses and abuses exercised by the Credit Mobilier erupted into one of the most publicized scandals of the nineteenth century. However, the dealings of those involved in Credit Mobilier had been well-known among insiders for years, and the smell of easy money had attracted legions of parasites and thieves to the Union Pacific camp.

WHICH WAY WEST?

While the devious Durant played political shenanigans in New York and Washington, his engineers explored the plains and mountains of the West searching for the best place to lay the railroad. By the 1860s, railroad engineering had matured into a respectable profession and there was more than a generation of knowledge of where the best places were to locate railroad lines. Union Pacific had equipped several teams of skilled engineers and surveyors to find the most cost effective route. Spending months hundreds of miles from civilization, riding around on horseback, and camping beneath the stars, they surveyed a variety of routes through the Rocky Mountain range. They carefully weighed the advantages, disadvantages, and costs of each possible route. There was considerable political sway involved in locating the best line. Newly formed Denver, Colorado—at the base of one of the most formidable portions of the Rockies—was one of the largest and fastest-growing communities in the West and hoped the transcontinental line would connect it with the eastern half of the nation. UP's surveyors considered a line to Denver and then over the Front Range of the Rockies but found such a prospect would be expensive and very time-consuming to build. Denver was disappointed when it learned that the UP chose a route 120 miles to the north. Likewise, Mormon leaders in Utah anxiously awaited the arrival of the railroad and

Cozad, Nebraska's, claim to fame is that is sits astride the 100th meridian. Union Pacific notes this on a special sign along the Overland Route main line at the handsome Cozad depot in 1978. *John Leopard*

encouraged Union Pacific to route its line west via Salt Lake City. They supplied UP survey teams with animals, guides, and equipment and played politics with Durant, but they too were ultimately disappointed when the railroad chose a route some 40 miles north of Salt Lake City.

Sam Reed was one of UP's most talented men, and through his vision, optimism, and hard work—and with the help of his assistants and Mormon guides—Union Pacific was able to locate a suitable path to the Great Salt Lake from the high plains of Wyoming. In the summer of 1864, Reed surveyed a line through the narrow confines of Weber and Echo canyons, places that would become some of the scenic highlights of UP's transcontinental route. Other surveyors had a more difficult time, confounded by difficult terrain, harsh weather, convoluted politics, and rightfully hostile tribes of American Indians.

Searching for a pass over the Rockies from the east had proved elusive and difficult. Climbing the Front Range out of Denver had been ruled out because the mountains were such a daunting barrier at this point. A route to the north through the Black Hills was also considered but was felt to be long and circuitous.

In 1865, General Dodge, as the railroad's new chief engineer, was exploring the Black Hills to the west of what is now Cheyenne, Wyoming, looking for the best path for the railroad. One afternoon, he and his men had strayed from the cavalry assigned to protect them and were surprised by a band of Indians. Dodge describes the fortuitous events that followed:

> " . . . I looked down into the valley [and] there was a band of Indians who had worked themselves in between our party and the [wagon] trains. I knew it meant trouble for us; they were either after us or our stock. I therefore immediately dismounted, and giving our horses to a couple of men with instructions to keep on the west side of the ridge out of sight and gunshot as much as possible, we took the ridge between Crow Creek and Lone Tree Creek, keeping it and holding the Indians away from us . . .
>
> "We made signals for our cavalry, but they did not seem to see them. It was getting along in the afternoon, as we worked down the ridge, that I began to discover we were on an apparently very fine approach to the Black Hills, and one of the guides has stated I said, 'If we saved our scalps, I believed we had found a railroad line over the mountains'"

Dodge and his party successful evaded the Indians, and months later Dodge sent another survey party led by James Evans to locate a

Photography was in its infancy (and color photography unimaginable) as the UP was building west in the 1860s, so scenes of conflict between Native Americans and the relentless railroad-builders had to be left to the imaginations of artists such as Howard Fogg, who did this Wild West scene for use on UP dining-car menu covers a hundred years later. *Union Pacific Museum Collection*

Two behemoths of UP transport—Big Boy steam locomotive No. 4011 and an 8,500-hp. gas-turbine—stand ready to serve in the Cheyenne station in the late 1950s. The spire atop UP's splendid depot building made it the tallest structure in Wyoming. Cheyenne itself was one of the railroad's most important division points and the junction of the Denver line with the Overland Route main line. *UP, David P. Oroszi collection*

railroad right-of-way over the pass, which he did. Dodge was very proud of this accomplishment and after Evans had secured the route, he said . . .

> ". . . This summit I immediately named for my old commander, General Sherman."

Sherman is at an elevation of 8,242 feet above sea level. When the Union Pacific completed its route through here, it proudly proclaimed that it had the highest tracks on earth. Since that time much higher lines have been built. Today the railroad crosses the pass at an elevation of 8,015 feet and the crossing is known as Sherman Hill. It is the highest point on the Overland Route, and although it is one of gentlest crossings of the Rockies, it was one of the most difficult sections to operate on Union Pacific's transcontinental line for many years. Sherman Hill, however, is not the crossing of the Continental Divide; this is accomplished at an elevation of just 7,107 feet at Creston, Wyoming, many miles farther west.

BUILDING WEST

Despite the revised Pacific Railroad Act, a multitude of problems slowed construction during the early years. The lack of a direct

railroad connection to Omaha/Council Bluffs area made the shipment of supplies slow and expensive. The Civil War resulted in a severe labor shortage and inflated the cost of workers and machines. But, it was Doctor Durant's own inept actions that proved one of the biggest impediments to progress. His egotistical, heavy-handed management and obvious self-serving attitude alienated many of his best employees and offended his potential allies. Durant's greed was notorious. For example he routinely ignored the advice of his top engineers regarding the most efficient railroad alignment and instead hired lackeys to survey circuitous routes that would guarantee more government subsidy and line his own pockets. Perhaps the most grievous instance was the famous Oxbow line immediately west of Omaha that added nine miles to Peter Dey's survey. Durant, desiring the longer route out of the Missouri Valley, ignored Dey's survey. He was motivated by the prospect of instant gratification through immediate subsidy, and the longer line gave him more options with eastern connections. But, Durant's selfish motives disgusted Dey who viewed the longer line as wasteful and greedy. Although Dey's superior alignment was ignored by Durant, it was the best route west, and not until nearly 40 years after the completion of the transcontinental route did UP finally built its Lane Cutoff along Dey's route west of Omaha.

Although initial progress moved at a glacial pace, by 1865 the railroad was actively moving west. What finally got the UP going was a clause of the Pacific Rail Act stipulating that if another line reached the 100th meridian first, it could be granted the transcontinental subsidy instead of the Union Pacific. So while Durant had foundered, stalled, and played political games, another line—later known as the Kansas Pacific—had organized to build west from Kansas City across the Kansas plains toward Denver. Durant realized that by dawdling, he risked losing the grants and subsidy that promised to make him a rich man. On July 10, 1865, before the KP could make any substantial progress, Union Pacific track-laying finally got underway and quickly proceeded across Nebraska. (Durant didn't wish to take any chances, though, and had purchased an interest in the Kansas Pacific route.)

The conclusion of the Civil War opened the labor market, and thousands of young men flooded west to work on the railroad. By 1866, Union Pacific rails had reached North Platte, Nebraska.

Hell on Wheels

The construction of the Union Pacific was one of the largest and most labor-intensive peacetime endeavors ever undertaken. It employed thousands of men to survey the route, grade the right-of-way, lay ties and track, and erect depots and other railway structures along the line. UP employed more

UP's engine terminal at Cheyenne was a great place to watch steel monsters of the prairies get fed and watered between runs. It's September 4, 1957, and Challenger 3966 awaits its next assignment while various gas-turbine locomotives stand nearby. *John Dziobko*

The locomotive that made Union Pacific (extra) famous: A Big Boy approaches the Colorado & Southern (Burlington) overpass and Cheyenne tower as it drifts into Cheyenne with an eastbound freight off of Sherman Hill in September 1957. *John Dziobko*

What a difference a dozen years make! At the same location as the top photo, but photographed from a higher vantage point, diesels now rule the Overland Route main line on July 4, 1969, as a huge westbound freight departs Cheyenne behind an all-Electro-Motive set of locomotives that include a GP9, GP20, DD35A, two GP9Bs, and an F7B. It's still no comparison to a Big Boy or Challenger storming out for Ogden, but a fascinating collection of motive power nonetheless. *Mike Schafer*

than just a few track gangs; it had a whole army of men. In addition to UP's own employees, concerns about Indian attacks brought along whole regiments of the U.S. Cavalry to protect the workers and the railroad from vandalism and violence.

Union Pacific's army was a notoriously wild bunch comprised of former Civil War soldiers, Irish immigrants escaping famine and British imperialism, freed black slaves, and a host of others seeking their fortune in the great American West. On the plains west of Omaha, the railroad builders were on the very edge of civilization where there were few laws and virtually no law enforcement. The U.S. was still

reeling from the most violent war in its history, and the memories of battles, death, and dying were still fresh in men's minds. Building the Union Pacific was dangerous work with few rewards. The men who did this work knew that each day may very well be their last, so when they were not working, they were living life to fullest in the ways they knew best. Certainly a scant few of them took life at leisure, reading great works of literature and honing their various crafts while carefully saving their earnings for their future, but the vast majority did not! Quite the contrary, when they were not working they drank, gambled, caroused, fought, and engaged in every sort of debauchery

Not all that many miles west of Cheyenne, the scenery suddenly becomes quite dramatic. In September 1992, a westbound dropping down the west slope of Sherman Hill winds among the "cowboy country" topography at Dale Junction, Wyoming, where the New Line joins the older Overland alignment. *David P. Oroszi*

23

known to man. Their wild, unrestrained antics both fascinated and horrified civilized people from the East known for their puritanical conservative values.

As the railroad moved west, boomtowns sprung up along the way to cater to the needs—and vices—of UP's army. These towns offered everything a hard-working man might want after a long day's labor. They were lined with saloons, dance halls, brothels, and theaters. This rolling, ephemeral debauchery attracted unsavory characters from every sphere, and gamblers, opportunists, thieves, pimps, and whores of all kinds made their way west seeking fortune and pleasure whether they worked for the railroad or not.

As the railroad moved, so did this support network. No sooner had a town boomed than it dried up. One day a town might have a population of 4,000 people and a week later it might have just 40, 400, or however many people decided to lay back and make the spot home. This was how cities such as North Platte, Julesburg, Cheyenne—all mobile towns, little festivals of wonder and vice—arose from barren prairies.

America was enthralled with this sideshow to the building of the Pacific Railroad and lapped up everything they could read about it. Samuel Bowles, the publisher of the Springfield (Massachusetts) *Republican*, traveled west to report on the progress of the railroad and the antics of its illustrious builders. In his travels, Bowles visited Benton, Wyoming, the latest haven for UP's motley army, declaring it "a congregation of scum and wickedness." He went on to sum up the entire enterprise, as "hell on wheels," a phrase which stuck in the minds of his readers. It seemed that reporters loved to condemn the lives of those that had

Big Boy 4022 has just come off the New Line (also known as the Harriman Line) at Dale Junction with a westbound train of mixed freight circa 1950. The scene on the previous page was taken from the hill at right in the background. Separated by this hill, the old and new lines join at the water tower partway back. Otto C. Perry, Denver Public Library, Western History Department

Eastbound (left in photo) and westbound freights pass on the high plains near Hermosa, Wyoming, in June 1986. *John Leopard*

At 6 P.M. on the evening of September 16, 1992, a westbound bounds out of Hermosa Tunnels and straight into the sunset. The tunnels take the Overland Route main line through a ridge some five miles west of Dale Junction. *David P. Oroszi* risked everything to build the transcontinental railroad. It wasn't enough to live at the edge of the earth, thousands of miles from family and friends, in a virtual void free from the comforts of home, performing back-breaking labor from dawn to dusk, but one should follow the pretense of a god-fearing wholesome existence too. Well, it didn't matter what the reporters wrote, since UP's army didn't have much time to read about it anyway.

Indians and the Railroad

The blind arrogance and self-proclaimed moral superiority of the railroad builders and their military protectors had little regard for the lives or culture of the Plains Indians, whose land they invaded and livelihood they ruined. To the railroad builders, the railroad represented a sort of holy quest, a classic battle of good and evil, and anyone who opposed it needed to be crushed. Likewise, the Plains

Indians were horrified at incursion of European settlers who were destroying the Buffalo herds that Indians depended on. They quickly developed an ardent hatred for the railroad and its builders. While some tribes accepted the whites and their railroad, others—notably the Cheyenne, Arapaho and the Sioux—fought the railroad invasion. The railroad and traditional Indian life simply could not coexist. For a few years, Indian warriors raged a guerrilla war against the Union Pacific and other lines pushing out on to plains. While many people were killed on both sides of this conflict, the perceived savagery of Indian attacks provoked harsh retaliation. The railroad builders had the backing of the United States military who ultimately overpowered the Indians. By 1868 the Army had given license to anyone with a gun to kill any Indians seen on or near railroad property. The conflict was resolved through force and oppression and within a few years of the completion of the Union Pacific, the Indians had been subdued and the attacks on the railroad ended.

RACE TO PROMONTORY

Union Pacific's army moved west across the plains following the North Platte River to the town of the same name. From there it ran along the South Platte River to Julesburg, Colorado, where it picked up Lodge Pole Creek, which it followed toward Cheyenne (the South Platte led to Denver). In July 1867, Cheyenne, 516 miles west of Omaha, was little more than a windswept oasis on the edge of the Black Hills. It was named for the Cheyenne Indians, one of several bands who had fiercely resisted the Union Pacific's westward progress. When the railroad arrived, Cheyenne's population swelled dramatically in a very short time, and a whole town seemed to magically materialize out of the sage brush. In his book *Hear that Lonesome Whistle Blow*, Dee Brown relates the impressions of Dr. Henry C. Perry who visited Cheyenne in 1867 as the Union Pacific was approaching:

> "When I left here last July all the land was bare, and the only habitations were tents. Cheyenne has now a population of fifteen hundred, two papers, stores, warehouses, hotels, restaurants, gambling halls, etc."

By the time the tracks and construction crews reached the town, more than 4,000 people were residing there. The price of property jumped dramatically as well. In July 1867 the railroad was selling 66 x 132-foot lots for $150; just 90 days later these same lots were offered at more than $2,000. Although Cheyenne's population would drop a bit when the Hell on Wheels continued farther west, it would fare far better than most. Union Pacific had selected Cheyenne as the site of a shop complex and as its junction with the Denver Pacific line south along the Front Range to Denver.

The division point of Green River, Wyoming, lies some 300 miles west of Cheyenne. In September 1992, a westbound grain train files past the landmark depot on which a yard tower has been added above the station portico. The main line to the Pacific Northwest junctions with the Overland Route main at Granger, 30 miles west, so Green River serves as a marshalling point for traffic destined for both routes. Likewise, during the later years of UP's passenger era, the *City of Portland* cars were split from the *City of Los Angeles/City of San Francisco* at Green River. *David P. Oroszi*

Continued on page 30

The red cliffs that loom above the Overland Route main line in Echo Canyon east of Ogden have long been a favorite photography location, for UP publicity photographers as well as railroad historians. Castle Rock dwarfs the two big General Electric units heading this east-bound in the summer of 1991. *Brian Jennison*

Continued from page 27

By the end of 1867 Union Pacific had reached from Cheyenne to Sherman Summit, but it still had a long way to go before reaching the Great Salt Lake. The pressure to build faster was intensifying as UP's Western counterpart Central Pacific was making good progress. What worried Durant was that Central Pacific, despite tough conditions, was making steady progress in the California Sierra range and would soon be racing eastward across the Nevada desert. Every mile the CP claimed east of the California-Nevada line was one fewer mile for Union Pacific, and that meant less subsidy for Durant. Furthermore, CP was aiming to reach the Mormon settlements along the eastern shore of the Great Salt Lake. If CP got there ahead of Union Pacific, it would secure that region's potentially lucrative traffic at UP's expense. In 1868, Union Pacific raced across Wyoming, reaching Echo Canyon, Utah, at the end of the year while CP rolled across Nevada as far as Carlin.

By 1869 both lines had sent survey and grading parties far ahead of their respective end of tracks. These parties overlapped and began grading parallel, duplicative lines, while fighting with one another. It was one of the first instances in the West where rival lines vied for the right to build—but it certainly would not be the last. It was utterly pointless for both railroads to build separate grades since they were intended to complement one another, not compete. Finally in the spring of 1869, a compromise was reached, and the two railroads agreed to build to Promontory Summit (not Promontory Point, as is often mistakenly cited), a few miles northwest of Ogden. Then Union Pacific would sell its line between Ogden and Promontory to CP, and the official junction would be relocated to Ogden.

THE GOLDEN SPIKE

At Promontory Summit—that distant, barren place situated northeast of the Great Salt Lake—the tracks at long last neared each other.

The fireman of GE gas-turbine No. 16 leading an eastbound freight out of Ogden hams it up as the train winds through Weber Canyon. It's July 1969, and the days are numbered for the "Big Blows." *Mike Schafer*

It must have seemed an eternity for those who built the tracks, having spent four years toiling in harsh conditions thousands of miles from home. Yet, many were amazed at the rapidity that the railroad overall had been constructed. Few people had really expected the Pacific Railroad would really reach completion while others had blindly optimistic hopes that the Pacific Railroad would be completed in time for the U.S. Centennial in 1876. Thus, nearly everyone was surprised when, in the spring of 1869, the two separate railroads were ready for joining.

As the moment of unification approached, both lines hoped to use the completion to their greatest public advantage, and they planned to show off their very best. The Golden Spike Ceremony was set for May 8, 1869. Despite good intentions, their plans were unavoidably altered, and the ceremony was postponed to May 10. UP Vice President Durant was delayed on his way west, first when his special train was held up by a mob of angry railroad workers demanding back wages and then later when heavy rains produced flash floods in eastern Utah. His finely decorated Pullmans destined for Promontory were

abandoned, and he relied on a common train, led by an ordinary engine numbered 119, to take him the rest of the way.

The gala spike ceremony—documented by several photographers including the famous A. J. Russell—has been shrouded in myth. It was a cold, clear afternoon, but reports on the details of the event vary greatly. Some 600 people were there, including a smattering of politicians and civic officials, soldiers from the 21st Infantry, including the Tenth Ward Headquarters Band, but all told it was a relatively small number considering the thousands involved in building the Pacific Railroad. Doctor Durant, General Grenville Dodge, and John "Jack" Casement—the man largely responsible for UP's construction—represented the Union Pacific. Central Pacific's president, Leland Stanford, was present along with Sam Montague, but most of CP's key players, including the notorious C. P. Huntington, were conspicuous by their absence.

Two trains, one from each railroad, posed pilot-to-pilot at their respective "ends of track." Track gangs laid the rails connecting the two railroads. A prayer was given, speeches

One hundred years prior to the photo on the facing page, numerous railroad workers and officials ham it up in one of the most famous scenes of U.S. history: the driving of the Golden Spike at Promontory Summit northwest of Ogden on May 10, 1869. Union Pacific 119 is at right. Shaking hands in the center are Sam Montague, the chief engineer of the Central Pacific (left), and Grenville M. Dodge, chief engineer of the Union Pacific. *UP, collection of David P. Oroszi*

Union Depot, Ogden, Utah.

were made, and then several commemorative spikes were gently taped into the last tie. Central Pacific's Leland Stanford was given the honor of placing the final gold spike—17.6 carats and nearly 6 inches long and bearing the words "The Last Spike"—into a pre-driven hole in a laurel oak tie. Because gold was too soft, this was not the spike that was driven in the traditional manner. For the final driving, a regular iron spike was used, but it was wired such that its contact with the head of the special mallet would send a telegraph signal to Chicago and Washington. Stanford sportingly gripped the ceremonial silver mallet, made a hearty swing at the spike, and missed! Durant then emulated Stanford's attempt, and likewise missed. When it was finally hit, the completed circuit triggered fire bells in Chicago and lowered a ball above the Capitol dome in Washington. At 12:47 P.M., a telegrapher relayed the message to the world: "Done!"

It was simply a symbolic action, but the Golden Spike Ceremony represented more the completion of just the railroad, it was uniting east with west. In honor of this achievement there were festive celebrations around the nation. Long parades, fireworks, and copious amounts of drink marked the moment in the minds off Americans everywhere. Even Wall Street paused to commemorate the moment. Poet Bret Harte expressed the significance of the Golden Spike in these words:

What was it the Engines said,
Pilots touching, head to head
Facing on the single track,
Half a world behind each back?
This is what the Engines said,
Unreported and unread.

DONE! WELL—NOT REALLY

That prophetic exclaim "Done!" hardly described the Union Pacific on May 10, 1869. Far from it, in fact. Although the tracks at Promontory Summit were linked, the railroad, particularly the Union Pacific, was far from completed. Perhaps the only thing that really was done was Doctor Durant's authority over the Union Pacific. By the time he swung his mallet, his control had effectively ended. He had been first forced out of Credit Mobilier in 1867 and then finally purged from control of the UP. While he lingered in the shadows for a few more years, he no longer controlled the pulse of the railroad.

One hundred years after the ceremony at Promontory Summit, E. Roland Harriman—E. H. Harriman's son and a member of Union Pacific's board of directors—estimated that it cost $90 million (in 1860s dollars) to build the railroad. But the Union Pacific was built in haste: speed, not quality, mattered. And who knows how much money was squandered and stolen by the likes of Durant and his cronies. Many sections of the railroad needed to be reworked before

government inspectors would authorize subsidy payments for construction.

Roughly six months passed before the railroad was fully ready to accommodate traffic—although through trains commenced shortly after the spike ceremony. One of the deficiencies had been the use of low-quality ties. To avoid paying the high cost of hardwood ties, Durant mandated the use of cottonwood instead. Many of these were burnettized, a process that compressed the wood and treated it with a zinc solution, which was intended to extend their life. But, by 1869, many cottonwood ties had already disintegrated and needed replacement. The grading was substandard too. Reports indicate that in some places, Union Pacific crews had laid track down on snow and frozen ground, so when spring thaws came, the tracks were rendered useless and had to be rebuilt.

The fledgling Union Pacific faced other serious problems too. The promise of enormous traffic flowing to the West Coast did not materialize overnight. In reality, in its early years the UP accommodated only a trickle of freight and passenger traffic . A single through passenger train and two freights in each direction sufficed to carry UP's transcontinental traffic. Initially, the UP set its rates extremely high, which had the effect of discouraging people from using the railroad.

Union Pacific's Ogden depot is shown undergoing a beautiful restoration job in 1981. At the time, the building was still being used as a passenger station for Amtrak. Note the mural above the ticket counter. *Mike Schafer*

The covers of this travel guide dating from 1931 illustrated the great advances made in Western transportation under the leadership of UP over the course of some 70 years. (But what would today's environmentalists say about the missing tree?) *Brian Solomon collection*

The Expansion Era

JAY GOULD AND EDWARD HARRIMAN HELP GROW AN EMPIRE

The Union Pacific was not in good shape when the transcontinental line opened, and in 1873 the railroad suffered further when the abuses of the Credit Mobilier became public, tarnishing the reputations of many of those involved with the railroad in its early years and associating the line with corruption and scandal. The Panic of 1873—the worst financial depression until that time and precipitated by the collapse of Jay Cooke and his Northern Pacific Railroad—decimated the price of UP stocks, allowing Jay Gould to pick it up for a bargain. Gould only controlled the Union Pacific for a short time, but under his influence the railroad was greatly expanded—as was Gould's wealth and influence. Many historians have criticized Gould's selfish aims and decried him for not investing in UP's upkeep and long-term welfare. It is widely believed that Gould's apparent profiteering contributed to the railroad's bankruptcy in the 1890s. However, Gould also provided guidance for the UP during a time of enormous change.

The dynamics of Western railroading evolved rapidly in the 1870s and 1880s, and the UP went from being the sole route to the West to one of several transcontinental corridors. By the mid 1880s, Union Pacific was facing competition from the Northern Pacific, Denver & Rio Grande Western, Atchison, Topeka & Santa Fe, Missouri Pacific, and its transcontinental partner, Central Pacific, which had control of the Southern Pacific—a line that had built another transcontinental route via Texas to New Orleans.

Under Gould's influence, the UP found the capital for expansion, and it built and acquired many new routes in a very short period of time. Expansion came at very high

cost and occurred at a time when the railroad's finances were strapped because of the heavy debt burden incurred during its early construction. Some historians have argued that the Union Pacific would have been better suited investing its money on its existing lines and paying down its onerous debts to the Federal government instead of building long extensions into new territory. Complicating the UP's tenuous situation, Gould variously worked for—and against—Union Pacific interests, depending on his own self-guided financial whims. He abandoned the Union Pacific in 1884, only to re-assume control in 1890; then he died two years later, leaving the railroad in financial shambles.

UNION PACIFIC EXPANSION

Utah Lines

The transcontinental railroad missed Salt Lake City, a fact that did not go unnoticed by Mormon leaders. One of UP's first branch lines was the Utah Central, which connected Salt Lake City with the main line at Ogden. This branch was built by Mormon interests who initiated work only a few days after the Golden Spike Ceremony at Promontory Summit. The Utah Central was completed by January 1870, and passenger service began on the 17th of that month. UP had an interest in the line from the start and ultimately took full control of the branch.

Mormon interests had their sights on reaching outlying settlements and also hoped to tap mineral resources in south central Utah, so they initiated the Utah Southern in January 1871. The railroad was built southward through the Utah Valley with Union Pacific support. It reached Provo in 1873, and by 1875 it terminated at York, a remote,

population-free spot some 73 miles south of Salt Lake City.

One of the most ambitious Utah projects was the Utah Northern, which was designed to run north of Ogden toward the mining districts in southwestern Montana. This company was incorporated by Mormon interests in August 1871 as a three-foot-gauge line, making it one of the first American narrow-gauge railways. Construction began in 1872 but proceeded slowly in the early years because of insufficient funding. The tracks reached Franklin, Utah, in 1874. Union Pacific saw the value in this route and lent its support. In 1878 the UN was reorganized as the Utah & Northern, but continued to suffer financially.

Although the promise of lucrative mineral traffic inspired the builders, they were incapable of realizing any revenue from this traffic until after the railroad reached the mining districts—a quandary faced by many branch feeders and secondary routes being built in the West. By 1880 the line crossed Monida Pass, and the tracks finally reached Butte, Montana,

in December 1881. Finally, on September 23, 1883, the Utah & Northern reached Garrison, Montana—385 miles from Ogden—arriving there only a couple of weeks after the Northern Pacific. Narrow-gauge operations made interchanging traffic difficult, and in 1887 part of the line was converted to standard gauge. Two years later Union Pacific merged it with its Oregon Short Line subsidiary (see pages 39–40) forming the Oregon Short Line & Utah Northern. A further consolidation in 1897 changed the name to the Oregon Short Line Railroad Company.

Kansas Pacific

Kansas Pacific's origins date to the early 1860s, and for a short time it was known as the Union Pacific Eastern Division—a confusing name because at that time the railroad had no corporate connection to the Union Pacific. In its early days, promoters of the Kansas Pacific route hoped it would become the eastern leg of the Pacific Railroad, but a sequence of unfortunate events conspired against that outcome. Instead, the KP became a transcontinental feeder, running west from Kansas City to Denver, with a connection to the Union Pacific at Cheyenne by way of the Denver Pacific. The western portion of the line was built under the direction of General William Jackson Palmer, one of the great railroad visionaries of the post-Civil War period. Upon completion of the KP, Palmer went on to build the narrow-gauge Denver & Rio Grande, which he hoped would link Denver and Mexico City.

The final 150 miles of the KP was constructed in less than four months at a rate of more than a mile day, an impressive accomplishment by any standard. In August 1870, the line reached Denver, then the largest settlement in Colorado Territory; six years later Colorado would become the 38th state. In the decade following the arrival of the railroad, Colorado's population jumped by an amazing 500 percent as settlers, prospectors, miners, and railroadbuilders flocked there, hoping to earn their fortune.

In its earlier years, the Kansas Pacific competed with Union Pacific for traffic, but it was stifled by the vast, lightly populated territory it traversed and its dependency on the UP for its westward connection. The line was perpetually in financial difficulties. In the late 1870s, Jay Gould took control of the KP, then, in a complex power play, he forced the consolidation of the two properties along with Denver Pacific. This move proved financially rewarding for Gould but did not necessarily help the UP. E. H. Harriman's biographer, George Kennan, explains the implications of the Union Pacific-Kansas Pacific combination:

> "By virtue of this consolidation, the mileage of the Union Pacific was nearly doubled; but its financial strength was very much weakened, the reason that the absorption of two unprofitable lines resulted in a large increase of capitalization without any commensurate increase in earning capacity. The Union Pacific had pried itself from competition, but at too high a cost, and its subsequent embarrassment and final insolvency were largely due to this taking in of the Gould roads at far more than their actual value."

Despite its financial drain, the Kansas Pacific proved useful to the Union Pacific in several ways. It no longer competed with UP and was kept out of the hands of stronger railroads that might be in a better position to rival UP. Furthermore, it gave UP better access to eastern connections via Kansas City, allowing UP to circumvent the "Iowa Pool"—the three principal railroads operating east of Council Bluffs—and put the UP in a much stronger position to negotiate rates and tariffs.

Following Union Pacific's acquisition of the Kansas Pacific and Denver Pacific, UP began to greatly expand its branchline network in an effort to tap more traffic, expand its territory, fend off potential competitors, and improve service. For example, in 1881 UP completed its route from Julesburg, Colorado, to Denver. As a through line, this route duplicated the Denver Pacific line via Cheyenne, which UP also controlled, but it dramatically cut running time between Denver and Omaha. Using this route, UP was able to offer passenger service between these two cities in just 24 hours.

After Gould relinquished his interest in Union Pacific in 1884, the railroad, then under the direction of Charles Francis Adams, continued its branchline expansion at an alarming rate. In just six years UP added some 3,000 new miles to its branchline network. The cost of these lines aggravated UP's debt problems despite providing the railroad with more originating traffic.

The UP reached Butte, Montana, in 1881 through the Utah & Northern, a railroad sponsored by—and later merged into—the UP through consolidation with another predecessor road. The U&N was never a high-volume route and for many years had but a single passenger train, the *Butte Special*. The Butte-to-Ogden train is shown in July 1970 at Butte, where it shared depots with the Northern Pacific. *Jim Heuer*

Colorado Lines

During the 1870s and 1880s, Colorado enjoyed a mining boom that saw a number of lines, mostly narrow gauge, built high into the Rockies to reach mining camps. Union Pacific was interested in tapping this potentially lucrative mine traffic and took control of several Colorado-based railroads. In 1879, it leased the mixed-gauge Colorado Central, which operated a three-foot-gauge line that connected Golden with Georgetown and Central City and ultimately reached all the way to Silver Plume. This line operated the famous Georgetown Loop, a spectacular track arrangement (now resurrected for tourists) featuring a complete 360-degree curve bringing the tracks up and over themselves within the narrow confines a of rocky canyon. Georgetown was the location of mines and was also a tourist destination from its early days.

In 1880, UP acquired control of the Denver, South Park & Pacific, another three-foot-gauge line which in July of that year had reached Leadville, the location of an extremely prosperous mining camp. Furthermore, the DSP&P was building west toward the Gunnison mining area. In 1881, UP consolidated the DSP&P as its South Park Division. This amazing narrow-gauge railroad crossed the Rockies through the fabled Alpine Tunnel at an elevation of 11,612 feet above sea level. Treacherous 4 percent grades combined with extremely heavy snowfall often made operations over this route prohibitively difficult. Alpine Tunnel was closed for years at a time because of snow.

In 1888 Union Pacific took an interest in lines building a route from Denver to Fort Worth, one of which was known as the Denver, Texas & Gulf. In 1890 it reorganized these lines along with the Colorado Central, Cheyenne & Northern, and other Colorado properties, except the South Park, to form the Union Pacific, Denver & Gulf. It was a

Electro-Motive F-units, a GP30, and a GP9B blaze their way south near Preston, Idaho, with a freight on the old Utah & Northern in July 1969. *Mike Schafer*

short-lived adventure, and the Panic of 1893 brought an end to most UP control of these Colorado-based lines.

Northwest Expansion

In the 1870s, the Pacific Northwest was virgin fertile territory. It was ripe, ready, and waiting for adequate transportation. Union Pacific had eyed this region since its earliest days. In the late 1860s, before the completion of the first transcontinental line, General Dodge had begun preliminary surveys for a line to the Northwest. The Northwest presented obvious expansion opportunities for the Union Pacific. California was the domain of Central Pacific interests, and the existing transcontinental line precluded any direct UP routes to that area. Meanwhile, Southern California and the Southwest were embroiled in a turf war between Southern Pacific and Santa Fe.

The Northwest by contrast had no railroads of consequence, although the Northern Pacific had been making noises for years about building to Washington. The lands in Idaho and Montana were known to be rich with valuable minerals, and the forests of Oregon and Washington were bountiful with choice timber. As a gateway to the Orient, Portland was willing to allow the UP to tap the Pacific Rim steamship trade directly, circumventing the Central Pacific. Despite the high promise for lucrative traffic, UP delayed building into the Northwest for nearly a decade because of its ongoing financial difficulties.

Finally, in 1879 Union Pacific organized its interests and moved to build a line toward Oregon. The Oregon Short Line was built under the guise of an independent line but in reality was a Union Pacific subsidiary from the beginning. It would connect with the UP main line at Granger, Wyoming, and follow the Snake River northwest into Idaho. In 1881 the OSL initiated construction and a year later reached 321 miles from Granger to Shoshone, Idaho. Here a branch was constructed northward toward Ketchum, Washington, to tap into mine traffic in the Wood River region. In this regard, UP's Northwest extension had significant advantage over the original transcontinental line and the Utah extensions. The OSL was not dependent on its western terminal for traffic, and there were a variety of lucrative traffic sources along the way allowing the railroad to generate revenue long before tracks were completed. By 1883, the OSL had roughly

420 miles of track in service, including the branch, and was already producing traffic for Union Pacific.

Meanwhile, Henry Villard, a well-known Portland-based financier of German birth, had organized the Oregon Railway & Navigation Company to build eastward from Portland along the Columbia River toward the Idaho mining districts. Villard was very familiar with railroading, the UP, and Jay Gould. A few years earlier he had been appointed as the receiver for the Denver extension of the Kansas Pacific and had a volatile go-around with Gould regarding the future of that financially strapped line. Villard hoped to interest the UP in his OR&N route but was not immediately successful.

The OR&N followed the south bank of the Columbia River to Umatilla, Oregon, then left the water-level profile of the river and cut inland toward Pendleton, Oregon. Here the main line split. One line was built northward toward Walla Walla, Washington, Grange City, and ultimately all the way to Spokane (which it reached in 1889). The other line was built over

Mixed train No. 117 pulls into Manhattan, Kansas, on the old Kansas Pacific on April 25, 1971. Carrying both passenger and freight cars (note the freight cars coupled to the end of the train), 117 spent all day working its way west along the KP from Kansas City to Denver. The rarely photographed run was discontinued when Amtrak began operations on May 1, 1971. *Jim Heuer*

the Blue Mountains to avoid a circuitous low-grade profile following the Columbia and Snake rivers, terminating on the Oregon-Idaho boarder at Huntington, Oregon. To reach this point, the line crossed three serious mountain grades, the most impressive being the 4,204-foot-high Kamela Summit in the Blue Mountains. At Huntington, the OR&N connected with UP's OSL route. The OSL had finally reached Huntington—404 miles southeast of Portland—in November 1884, and a last spike ceremony was staged on on the 25th of that month. A week later, regular service began.

By the time the OR&N joined rails with the OSL, Villard's railroad scheme has taken on a whole new dimension. He had acquired control of UP's Northwest rival, the Northern Pacific, and in 1883 pushed that line through to a connection with his OR&N at Wallula Junction (near Pasco and the confluence of the Columbia and Snake rivers in eastern Oregon). This had diverted the NP from its original goal of a terminal near Tacoma, Washington, to a terminal at Portland, Oregon, where Villard's primary interests lay. It also gave NP the jump on the

UP in the Pacific Northwest.

Villard's finances had been weakened by the cost of building the NP, and he soon faltered and lost control of his infant railroad empire. His loss was UP's gain, and by 1887 UP had taken control of the OR&N and made it a subsidiary of the OSL. Meanwhile, the NP continued west on its own and built a line over Stampede Pass to reach Seattle and Tacoma.

Under Union Pacific control, the OR&N continued to build branch lines and connected many towns in the "Inland Empire" of eastern Washington and northeastern Oregon. The OSL built numerous feeders in southern Idaho. As a result, the whole region flourished and fed a variety of traffic to the Union Pacific. A healthy agricultural base, augmented by mineral traffic and a growing livestock trade, provided the UP a strong traffic foundation. In addition, the railroad tapped the oriental steamship trade as had been hoped.

As the railroad prospered, it continued to build new lines in the region while at the same time consolidating existing properties. In August 1896, Union Pacific consolidated its Oregon Railway & Navigation Company with

UP's stately depot in Seattle, Washington, was built by predecessor Oregon-Washington Railway & Navigation Company. This postcard is postmarked 1911. Though no longer used by passenger trains, the depot still stands but is more commonly known as Seattle Union Station. *Mike Schafer collection*

Far from home rails, a Conrail locomotive trails a UP SD40–2 on an eastbound freight at Perry, Oregon, in 1994. *Don Marson*

41

the Oregon Railway Extension Company and the Washington & Idaho Railroad into a new company called the Oregon Railroad & Navigation Company. In 1910, a further consolidation changed the name of the railroad to the Oregon-Washington Railway & Navigation Company. By this time the railroad operated nearly 1,500 miles of track in the region, of which it owned 1,143 miles.

THE HARRIMAN ERA

Edward Henry Harriman was one of the most dynamic men to ever grace American railroading. He was only involved with railroads for a relatively short time, but implemented many changes that guided the properties he controlled for decades after he

was gone. Today, he remains one of the best-remembered and highly regarded railroad leaders, and he built his reputation largely on his spectacular handling of the Union Pacific.

The Panic of 1893 precipitated the Union Pacific's bankruptcy, declared in October of that year. A number of problems, including the repayment of 30-year government bonds contributed to UP's financial woes. As the railroad's finances deteriorated, the system that had been built up by Durant, Gould, and others over the preceding three decades began to unravel at an alarming rate. The Denver Pacific, Kansas Pacific, the Colorado branches, the Oregon Short Line, and other extremities were stripped from the UP. By 1897, there was little left to the company

outside of its original transcontinental trunk. It was in this lone property that E. H. Harriman began to take interest in 1897. Despite the dubious attitude of Wall Street, which viewed the Union Pacific as a tenuous property, and the outward hostility of some long-time Union Pacific board members toward Harriman, he secured control of the railroad in 1898 and in a very short time he turned the company around, amazing Wall Street observers, UP stockholders, and life-long railroaders alike.

Harriman had learned about railroading running the Illinois Central, and he took his experience with the IC and applied it to the Union Pacific. Unlike many railroad executives who dealt strictly with finances and "big

picture" decision-making, leaving the details of actual railroad operation to subordinates, Harriman took exceptional interest in the details of daily railroad operation. His thorough knowledge of railroading gave him the insight and experience necessary to make the UP one of the finest properties in America, and it also earned him the respect of his employees, investors, and fellow railroad executives.

Once he was in control of the railroad, he made a calculated study of it, examining every element of its operations by talking to his employees a great length, quizzing them for information. Harriman was interested in all aspects of operations from a technical standpoint, and once he had put together a satisfactory picture of the Union Pacific, he was able to give very specific orders on how to improve the railroad as a whole. He acted swiftly and comprehensively, infusing capital and resources where he saw fit.

A common myth regarding Harriman's control of the Union Pacific would lead one to believe he took over a run-down line with virtually no hope for the future and amazingly turned it around in no time at all. The "two streaks of rust" crossing the Nebraska plains is a myth often repeated by historians who glorify Harriman but know little about railroading. Railroad author and historian Maury Klein has dispelled this inaccurate image of the pre-Harriman UP, pointing out that the railroad was in remarkably good condition when Harriman took over and was a fairly typical Western railroad of the period. What Harriman did do was elevate the railroad by improving the standard of its physical plant and vastly improve its ability and capacity to haul goods. So, he didn't just fix up a badly run down line that had suffered from years of neglect; he took a decent property with good prospects and made it into one of the best railroads in America. As Harriman's biographer, George Kennan, relates,

> "...Mr. Harriman wanted—as he said to his engineers and contractors—the best-built and best-equipped railroad that skill could devise and money pay for."

Kennan outlines Harriman's improvement strategy:

> "... by reducing grades, eliminating curves, and increasing the size of cars and the tractive power of locomotives, he expected not only to lessen the road's operating expenses, but to double its carrying capacity."

Harriman believed in the power of the Union Pacific and the potential of the

Oregon's Blue Mountains stand as a barrier to UP's main line between the Idaho-Oregon border and the Columbia River, which forms the boundary between Oregon and Washington. UP both circumnavigated and crossed the mountain range with two different lines. This eastbound freight near Kamela, Oregon, is on one of the three severe grades on the mountain-climbing main once used by the *City of Portland*. The beautiful scenery was a great draw for passengers, but wicked on freight traffic. *Brian Solomon*

It's a July evening at Pocatello, Idaho, in 1969 as the westbound *City of Portland* drifts into town following is day-long trek from Denver through eastern Colorado and southern Wyoming. At Granger, the train swung on to the old Oregon Short Line and eventually entered Idaho. Later in the evening and in the early morning hours of the following day, the famous streamliner will cross the Blue Mountains and by daybreak be skimming along the Columbia River toward its namesake city for a mid-morning arrival. When Amtrak was operating on this route, the Blue Mountains were crossed westbound in the morning. *Mike Schafer*

For nearly 200 miles, mainline trains of the old OSL-OR&N route to and from Portland follow the majestic Columbia River. This trio of GE locomotives have a westbound stack train in tow in the Columbia River Gorge at Blalock, Oregon, in April 1989. *John Leopard*

American West, and he had no qualms putting his money behind his vision. In just a short time after he had taken control of the railroad, he had regained control of most its tributaries and limbs torn from the trunk by bankruptcy. The Kansas Pacific, Denver Pacific, and OSL were soon back in the UP fold. He also recovered many of the various branch lines. One piece of the system that did not rejoin the UP was the Union Pacific & Gulf. Harriman salvaged the Julesburg–Denver route, too, but the rest of the lines became the Colorado & Southern, a line that eventually came under control of the Chicago, Burlington & Quincy.

His program of physical improvement began soon after he took control and continued throughout his 11-year reign over the railroad. The plan he mapped out for railroad improvement outlived him, and years after his death his vision was still being carried out. On the main line between Omaha and Ogden, Harriman implemented numerous line relocations to eliminate curvature and reduce gradient and mileage, correcting deficiencies incurred by the haste of the original builders and by the primitive construction techniques used in the 1860s. Author Klein estimates that Harriman's reconstruction shortened the main line by 54 miles and removed 26 complete circles' worth of curvature. Kennan indicates that in doing this, Harriman abandoned roughly 150 miles of UP's original main line—more than 10 percent of the original 1860s alignment. In addition to these improvements, he replaced wooden bridges and antique iron ones with new, stronger, steel bridges capable of accommodating greater loads with less maintenance. Also, the main line was upgraded with better ballast and heavier rail, and the majority of the Omaha–Ogden transcontinental main line was converted from single to double track. Between 1898 and 1909 Harriman spent nearly $175 million on improvements to the Union Pacific alone.

A westbound train of mixed freight sweeps around Leonard Horseshoe Curve east of Oxman, Oregon, in June 1993. At this point, the train is out of the Blue Mountains, but the topography will remain rugged from here to Portland. *Brian Solomon*

45

Another key to the railroad's revamping was the widespread employment of block signals. As of the turn of the century, the rear-end collision had become one of the most common types of fatal railroad accidents. In 1900, Illinois Central locomotive engineer Casey Jones lost his life in a widely celebrated rear-end collision. Two years later, a violent rear-end collision in the smoke-filled Park Avenue tunnel leading to New York City's Grand Central Station made headlines for weeks and infuriated the public. One of Harriman's interests was in railroad safety, and after these dramatic events he made a concerted effort to equip his lines with state-of-the-art automatic block signaling—specifically developed to protect against rear-end collisions. He became a leader in new signaling installations, setting the standard for American railway safety. By the time of Harriman's death in 1909, more than 5,000 route-miles of UP lines were equipped with automatic block signals, representing roughly 40 percent of all ABS installations in the U.S. at that time. Harriman's preferred signaling equipment were Union Switch & Signal "lower-quadrant" semaphores which became a symbol of safety on his lines.

SOUTHERN PACIFIC ACQUISITION

Harriman wasn't content with control of the Union Pacific and was soon eyeing the Central Pacific, which he believed was the natural extension of UP's original transcontinental main line. He approached the aged C. P. Huntington—the last of the original "Big Four" who had built and operated both the Central

Precipitous lava-rock walls along the Columbia River prompted the UP to take on some tunnelwork to reduce the snakelike path followed by the original OR&N alignment. This eastbound freight near The Dalles, Oregon, is punching through a bore that was opened in 1922. *Alex Mayes*

On two occasions during the twentieth century, the UP has made drastic alterations to its climb over Sherman Hill west of Cheyenne. Big Boy 4017 toils with a coal train in October 1958 on the New Line (or "Harriman Line") south of the earlier alignments over Sherman. This single-track bypass had been open for only five years. *Union Pacific Museum Collection, image No. SFA-233*

The Borie Cutoff and the Harriman Line

Union Pacific enjoys one of the easiest paths west. However, once it reaches Cheyenne, Wyoming, it faces the formidable barrier of the Black Hills. Although not as rugged as the Rockies and certainly not as difficult as other Western crossings, the Black Hills are legendary. It was here that General Dodge yarned about being chased by hostile Indians, a fortuitous incident that led him to find a suitable railway crossing. Dodge named his "discovery" in honor of his Civil War commander, General Sherman. It is still known as Sherman Hill on the Union Pacific.

Dodge's 1860s survey presented a practical way west in the early days of the UP, but the difficult climb over Sherman Hill plagued railroad operations. When E. H. Harriman took control in the 1890s, he set out to rebuild the railroad, and Sherman Hill was the focus of his earliest efforts. Harriman provided UP's Chief Engineer Berry with the resources to build a better way west over Sherman Hill. Between 1899 and 1903 Berry directed an army of laborers, steam shovels, and blasting teams to cut a new, more efficient path between Cheyenne and Hermosa. Where the old line closely followed the profile of the land, the new route used deep cuts, high fills, combined with an 1,800-foot-long summit tunnel. The crossing of Dale Creek alone required a massive 900-foot-long fill. When the new route was opened, it was considered one of the largest engineering endeavors of the age. It had chopped 247 feet off Sherman Summit, lowering it to just 8,014 feet above sea level.

The ruling westward grade on the new line, known as the Borie Cutoff, was just 1.55 percent (a climb of 1.55 feet for every 100 traveled). However, the Borie Cutoff over Sherman Hill was just one of many significant line relocations on the Overland Route implemented by Harriman. During World War I, the Borie Cutoff was double tracked.

Fifty years after the construction of the Borie Cutoff, Union Pacific set out again to improve its crossing of Sherman Hill and built a third track over this crucial pass. This line was designed to augment, rather than supplant, the 1903 Borie Cutoff. It was laid out as a low-grade route to ease the climb for heavy westbound freights. The route diverges from the old main line at Corlett Junction, a mile or so west of Cheyenne. It is not adjacent to the older line, and dips south following a sinuous path to maintain a steady 0.82 percent climb. The route is characterized by very deep cuts and long high fills, and some 7 million cubic yards of earth, stone, and debris were moved in its construction. It rejoins the old line at Dale Junction, just east of the Dale Creek crossing. The 1953 route is 42.5 miles long, making it nine miles longer than the earlier crossing, but it provides a much easier path for long trains. The 1953 line passes through Harriman, a place not named for the legendary E. H. Harriman, but his son Roland Harriman who was Union Pacific's Board Chairman in the early 1950s at the time of construction. Today, Sherman Hill's three tracks represent one of the busiest mountain crossings in the world.

and Southern Pacific railroads—with an offer to purchase the CP but was staunchly refused. This did not dissuade Harriman from pursuing his vision of a unified Union Pacific-Central Pacific, and when Huntington died in 1900, Harriman was quick to take control of not only the CP, but the entire Southern Pacific.

At that time the, SP was a comprehensive network and considered the largest transportation system in the world. Upon buying it, Harriman uttered his most-remembered words, "We have bought not only a railroad,

While many folks might assume the Nevada desert to be ironing-board flat, this scene in Meadow Valley Wash on the old Los Angeles & Salt Lake route proves otherwise. This eastbound is at Vigo, Nevada, in 1997. *Brian Solomon*

but an empire." Harriman gave the SP the same attention that he was giving the Union Pacific and immediately began upgrading the railroad to his high standards.

THE LOS ANGELES & SALT LAKE ROUTE

Union Pacific interests had long considered building a railroad southwest across Utah and Nevada into California to connect the Overland Route and Salt Lake City with Los Angeles. By 1880, UP tracks had reached 277 miles from the main line at Ogden to Frisco, Utah, to tap iron-ore deposits there. In the 1880s and 1890s, UP dispatched survey parties and grading teams to build a line through Clover Creek Canyon and the Meadow Valley Wash in southern Nevada, but the railroad's weak financial condition precluded it from finishing this work, and the work stalled before much track was laid.

At the turn of the century, a competing interest, led by Montana mining mogul Senator William A. Clark, pushed to build a railroad along this route. Clark secured property in the Los Angeles Basin, and after C. P. Huntington died, Clark chartered his San Pedro, Los Angeles & Salt Lake route (SPLA&SL). He negotiated running rights out of the Los Angeles Basin via Cajon Pass on the Santa Fe. Clark's aspirations aroused Harriman's interest, who for a short time competed with Clark to build a line to Los Angeles. In places they graded duplicative rights-of-way and battled in court for the authority to build a railroad. Finally, in 1902 they agreed to work together on the line, and UP took a 50 percent interest in the SPLA&SL. The route was completed in 1905.

Although the line was securely in the Union Pacific camp, it retained considerable independence as long as Senator Clark retained interest in the property.

HARRIMAN BATTLES FOR CONTROL OF THE WEST

Harriman had his eye on other properties in his continuing attempt to dominate transportation in the West. He vied for control of the Pacific Northwest with James J. Hill, the visionary mogul behind the Great Northern, and he battled with the Santa Fe for domination of the Southwest. Harriman attempted to secure control of the Burlington and later the Northern Pacific, but was foiled by Hill and Hill's notorious financier, J. P. Morgan. During this time, Harriman did manage to secure an entrance for UP into the growing ports of

Seattle and Tacoma while Hill built his Spokane, Portland & Seattle, giving Hill's Great Northern and Northern Pacific direct access to Portland. Hill and Harriman interests continued this battle for regional control by building into central Oregon along the Deschutes River. Ultimately they made a truce and jointly operated the Oregon Trunk route, with Union Pacific operating as far south as Bend, Oregon. Ultimately, GN used this line as part of a route that reached all the way to a connection with the Western Pacific in Northern California, but this was completed years after both Harriman and Hill had passed from the scene.

THE EMPIRE IS SEPARATED

In 1906, the Federal Government initiated an investigation into Harriman's properties just as Harriman became embroiled in a public feud with his one-time friend, President Theodore Roosevelt. By 1908 the investigation had escalated into an effort by the Federal government to separate UP and SP. As this move was gaining strength, Harriman's health faltered. He became extremely ill in December 1908, and despite efforts to rejuvenate his energy, he continued to weaken. He died in September 1909. It is said that on the day of his funeral, trains all across his vast system paused for a minute as a gesture of respect.

In 1912, the courts ruled to separate Union Pacific and Southern Pacific, an action that had the effect of turning two railroads that had been jointly run for more than a decade into competitors. Union Pacific sued in an effort to secure the Central Pacific route into California, and court battles ensued for another decade, but in the end—at least until the 1990s—Southern Pacific retained control of the CP transcontinental route.

Most *City of Los Angeles* passengers were asleep when their train was slipping through beautiful Clover Creek Canyon west of Barclay, Nevada, on the LA&SL (unless their train was terribly late). However, the crew of his westbound freight in March 1997 is enjoying the topography under the bright sun of a Nevada afternoon. *Brian Solomon*

Where Southern Pacific *Daylight* streamliners once paraded, Armour yellow diesels now hustle freight. A Los Angeles-bound double-stack train descends Santa Susana Pass near Chatsworth, California, on the former-SP Coast Line route in October 1998. Earlier in its history, UP and SP were closely aligned, but merger attempts were thwarted. Decades later, through an ironic twist involving a failed SP-Santa Fe merger attempt, Union Pacific wound up with the SP after all in 1996. *Alex Mayes*

3

THE OVERLAND ROUTE

Modern Era
Union Pacific

THE TRANSITION FROM UP'S "CLASSIC ERA" TO A NEW
RAILROAD OF THE LATE TWENTIETH CENTURY

In the seven decades that followed the separation from Southern Pacific, Union Pacific experienced very few changes to its basic system, although there were a number of internal adjustments and consolidations. The San Pedro, Los Angeles & Salt Lake was officially shortened to the Los Angeles & Salt Lake in 1916, and in 1921 UP bought out Senator Clark's share of the LA&SL. On January 1, 1936, UP consolidated its major railroad subsidiaries, including the Oregon Short Line, Oregon-Washington Railway & Navigation Company, and LA&SL into the Union Pacific system (although these lines remained as wholly owned subsidiaries until 1987).

The railroad's freight traffic grew and evolved while its passenger traffic ebbed and flowed with changes in American travel habits. UP handled enormous volumes of traffic during both world wars and weathered the Great Depression better than many American lines. During World War II, Union Pacific implemented Centralized Traffic Control on the LA&SL west of Las Vegas, Nevada, to streamline dispatching procedures, facilitate more efficient train movements, and increase capacity. This heavily graded single-track route was near capacity using conventional dispatching methods, and CTC proved the most economical answer to increasing track capacity quickly in order to accommodate the deluge of wartime traffic. After World War II, the railroad embarked on a major improvement plan, investing tens of millions of dollars in the railroad. Yards were upgraded and modernized while hundreds of miles of CTC was installed on both single- and double-track routes. Beginning in 1947,

Union Pacific made a concerted effort to dieselize its freight operations and bought hundreds of new diesels.

In 1958, the UP acquired control of the Spokane International, a 150-mile line running from Spokane, Washington, to Eastport, Idaho—the latter on the Canadian border—where it connected with the Canadian Pacific. The line was built in the early part of the twentieth century and commenced operations in 1906. When UP took control, the railroad had a fleet of 12 Alco RS1 diesels and slightly more than 200 freight cars.

Union Pacific was among the last American railroads to discontinue heavy steam operations, and on November 20, 1961, UP introduced post-steam-era excursions using its last 4-8-4, No. 844. Its steam excursions proved extremely popular and have continued on and off ever since. Over the last 30 years, UP has demonstrated its interest in railway preservation by collecting and maintaining a variety of vintage equipment for what it calls its Historic Fleet.

THE ROCK ISLAND DEBACLE

Following the Spokane International purchase, UP soon embarked on a more aggressive acquisition, the Chicago, Rock Island & Pacific. The plan drew numerous protests from other railroads, and the Interstate Commerce Commission dragged its heels on the approval study for many years. The ICC finally approved the union on November 8, 1974, but the decision had taken so long that the Rock had deteriorated physically and financially, and the UP no longer felt it was worth acquiring. UP officially declined the merger

Continued on page 56

Unlike many railroads who deem it necessary to shun their pasts, Union Pacific has long maintained a strong sense of heritage. Ties to its rich past remain through a number of venues, including occasional appearances of two remaining active members of its once-huge steam locomotive fleet. UP 4-8-4 No. 844 has an excursion train in tow on the railroad's former Missouri Pacific, nee Chicago & Eastern Illinois main line at Shoal Creek, Illinois, in June 1990. *Alex Mayes*

Five six-axle Electro-Motive units get a roll on symbol freight TACRD-02's (Tacoma–Conrail) 6,554 feet worth of K-Line containers coming out of the siding at Waterfall, Wyoming, on August 4, 1996. *Tom Kline*

three months later. This proved fatal to the Rock Island, which declared bankruptcy on March 17, 1975, and ceased all operations on March 31, 1980. Unlike many railroad bankruptcies, the Rock Island was not reorganized. Rather, it was dismembered and its lines and rolling stock sold off. Some routes were abandoned, but many were picked up by other railroads. Union Pacific bought a number of former Rock Island locomotives and ultimately acquired several key Rock Island routes through later mergers. Had Union Pacific acquired the Rock Island on its original schedule, there would likely have been a very different sequence of events in Western—and Midwestern—railroad history.

EVOLUTION OF THE MODERN UNION PACIFIC

In 1980, Union Pacific initiated an acquisition of both the Missouri Pacific (MoPac), and Western Pacific (WP), just as UP's primary railroad competitor, Burlington Northern, was consummating its merger with the St. Louis-San Francisco Railway—the Frisco—a 4,653 line connecting various cities in Missouri, Kansas, Oklahoma, Arkansas, Texas, Mississippi, and Alabama. BN had been formed a decade earlier as a result of a merger between properties once controlled by

Technically, it's the UP, but it still looks for all the world like the Chicago & North Western at Grinnell, Iowa, crossing the former Rock Island main line on June 12, 1995. The venerable C&NW had long been regarded as logical merger partner and a natural extension of the UP east of Omaha. For a time in the 1960s, it looked as though Rock Island would get that honor, though, but in the strange twists of U.S. railroad history, MoPac became the chosen one—and then the North Western, in the spring of 1995. *John Leopard*

UP finally got its coveted reach into the San Francisco Bay Area through the 1982 acquistion of the storied Western Pacific. An eastbound freight crosses the North Fork bridge in California's Feather River Canyon in May 1990. This breathtaking canyon was once the domain of the famous Burlington-Rio Grande-Western Pacific transcontinental domeliner *California Zephyr*, which WP operated between Salt Lake City and Oakland. Today's Amtrak *CZ* plies the former SP Donner Pass route to the south— a line to the Bay Area that UP would also eventually get in 1996. *Brian Solomon*

The UP influence is evident of this view of a southbound Missouri Pacific freight at Pilot Point, Texas, in 1985—but so is MP influence. The trailing locomotive may be painted Armour yellow, but it's lettered for Missouri Pacific. *John Leopard*

James J. Hill: Great Northern; Northern Pacific; Burlington; and Spokane, Portland & Seattle. UP's interest in acquiring the MoPac and WP was a reaction to the growing power of BN as well as to the deregulatory environment stimulated by the Staggers Act of 1980. This legislation freed American railroads from stifling rate regulations that had been in place for decades, allowing them to compete in areas they could not have touched before and yet permitting them to drop a variety of unprofitable operations and services.

The Union Pacific + Missouri Pacific + Western Pacific merger, referred to tongue-in-cheek by some industry wags as the "Mop-Up," was approved by the ICC in 1982, and the railroads were merged on December 22 of that year. The WP gave Union Pacific a long-coveted direct route into Northern California, allowing it to shift the bulk of its Overland traffic away from the traditional SP interchange at Ogden. The 3,130-mile-long Missouri Pacific, connected with UP at several locations, including Omaha and Kansas City,

An eastbound American President Lines stack train treads its way slowly along Third Street in Oakland in April 1993. This former WP main line has since been closed and the trains shifted to parallel ex-SP tracks (which also plie the streets of Oakland). *Brian Solomon*

Continued from page 52

and provided UP access to a host of new markets in Kansas, Missouri, Illinois, Oklahoma, Arkansas, Louisiana, and Texas. Although the Western Pacific quickly vanished into the Union Pacific, the MoPac retained elements of its corporate identity for several years after the merger. Locomotives continued to bear MoPac lettering, yet wore Union Pacific's corporate colors. The MoPac was not legally absorbed until March 1, 1997.

Union Pacific continued to expand in the late 1980s and 1990s. In May 1988, UP's Missouri Pacific subsidiary bought the 3,130-mile Missouri-Kansas-Texas Railroad, universally known as the "Katy." By the end of the year,

Katy's operations had been melded with that of UP. Meanwhile, the ailing Southern Pacific, which had been jettisoned by the Santa Fe following the ICC's rejection of their proposed merger, was purchased by Rio Grande Industries. This resulted in an effective merger between the two companies. The SP name was retained, while Rio Grande and SP's Cotton Belt subsidiary were de-emphasized.

In 1989, UP purchased a 25 percent interest in its longtime Midwestern interchange partner, Chicago & North Western. Then in the mid-1990s, the Western railroad scene entered merger frenzy. In 1994 Burlington Northern made a bid for Santa Fe, which provoked

Having departing Memphis, Tennessee, only minutes earlier, a westbound train of mixed freight eases off the Mississippi River bridge into West Memphis, Arkansas. There's little evidence of MP in this 1992 scene. *Alex Mayes*

Union Pacific to make a competing bid. By early 1995, UP gave up on its effort to acquire Santa Fe, but it had effectively driven up the price of the railroad for BN. Then, UP outright purchased the C&NW in the spring of 1995. In September, UP announced that it intended to acquire Southern Pacific (along with the former Rio Grande and Cotton Belt). This enormous controversial merger proposal spurred a complex debate regarding railroad competition in the West that was ultimately settled by UP providing BNSF with extensive trackage rights over many of its lines. The UP-SP merger was thus approved by the new regulatory agency, the Surface Transportation Board,

The Electro-Motive GP40X leading this passenger special over the Western Pacific between Oakland and Stockton in 1985 pays tribute to the dearly departed "Wobbly"—as the Western Pacific was affectionately known to its followers— through a WP herald attached to the locomotive front. *Sean Zwagerman*

The Missouri-Kansas-Texas Railroad still has a couple of years of life left as one of its long drag freights heads west out of Kansas City in 1986. By the end of 1988, the "Katy" would be another flag to fall in the sweep of mergers that eventually would make UP the largest railroad in North America. *Steve Smedley*

which had replaced the Interstate Commerce Commission a few months before the UP-SP case came up for review. What was different in this proposed second union than when UP-SP had been forcibly separated in 1912 was that the two had since been joined with several former competitors—namely the MP, WP, and D&RGW—as well as large portions of the Rock Island that earlier had been acquired by SP and C&NW. Also, where the railroad was the dominant form of transportation in the West in 1912, it now faced extensive competition from the highway and airline industry. Further, with trackage rights offered its primary rail competitor, UP-SP no longer appeared as a monopoly in the eyes of Federal regulators.

The merger was approved in July and went into effect on September 11, 1996. So, 90 years after the government first began investigating Harriman's properties, and 84 years after they were separated in court, his Western railroads were again joined as one unified company, becoming the largest railroad in the U.S.

A pair of GE locomotives drown out the drone of nearby Interstate 80 as they hoist an auto-rack train over the Sierra near Emigrant Gap, California, in the summer of 1999. This was Southern Pacific's end of the Chicago–Oakland Overland Route for well over a century while Chicago & North Western was the east-end anchor. Now, UP owns the whole Overland Route. *Alex Mayes*

Shortly after the UP-C&NW merger, the mixture of both road's locomotives became a common sight, as this scene at Clinton, Iowa, in 1995 attests.
Brian Solomon

It could pass as the *City of Portland* in 1957, but in reality this is a coal shippers' special climbing toward Soldier Summit, Utah, on the former Rio Grande main line in 1997. UP maintains a modest but impressive pool of its passenger equipment—including a set of rebuilt E-unit passenger diesels— for business and excursion use. *Alex Mayes*

Where boxcar, stock, and perishable trains once ruled, intermodal and coal are now king. A trio of GE locomotives sweep along the New Line near Tie Siding, Wyoming, west of Cheyenne with an eastbound intermodal train in 1992. Although the profit margin tends to be slim on intermodal traffic, and on-time performance is paramount, intermodal nonetheless is a key traffic base on the Union Pacific as well as on most of its contemporaries. Freight trains carrying general freight with traditional boxcars, gondolas, and the like still ply U.S. rails, including those of UP, but not in the numbers they used to. *Don Marson*

Be Specific— Ship Union Pacific

MOVING FREIGHT ON THE UP, THEN AND NOW

Over the years, the nature of Union Pacific freight traffic has evolved and grown. At one time, agricultural traffic including fruits, vegetables, and livestock represented a significant portion of UP's eastbound freight. Today this traffic has largely vanished, while intermodal moves and coal traffic has reached new records. Small shipments of single cars and less-than-carload traffic has been eclipsed by large bulk moves, unit trains, and dedicated TOFC (trailer-on-flatcar or "piggyback") and container runs.

PERISHABLE TRAFFIC

It is a crisp winter morning in 1944 in Utah's Weber Canyon. The ground shudders as a brand new Big Boy marches up between the cleft in the hills with a heavy train of 68 orange-and-white Pacific Fruit Express cars carrying fresh fruit and vegetables. This train is just one of a half dozen "Fruit Blocks" that will roll east from Ogden and cross the Union Pacific this day.

So stated the copy for a publicity scene on the UP being promoted during World War II. Unlike most freight trains, if a perishable train takes too long to reach its destination, its load becomes valueless. This makes it mandatory that perishable trains receive lots of extra of attention and that they maintain tight, expedited schedules to get fresh produce to its destination without spoiling.

The advent of insulated box cars—called refrigerator cars or reefers—combined with fast freight schedules permitted the successful transport of perishable goods. Reefers carried loads of fresh carrots, beans, cantaloupes, celery, and lettuce—produce that less than a week before was still growing in California and a week hence would be entirely consumed by people living everywhere from Minneapolis to New York City.

Pacific Fruit Express owned, maintained, and serviced a huge pool of refrigerator cars. PFE was formed under E. H. Harriman in 1906 and jointly owned by Union Pacific and Southern Pacific. It was one of the few Harriman joint institutions that survived the antitrust separation of UP and SP in the wake of Harriman's death. Despite the ensuing fight between the two railroads for domination of transcontinental traffic, PFE thrived.

Originally PFE operated and maintained just 6,000 40-foot insulated refrigerator cars. Initially these cars were only operated during harvest booms, but as PFE expanded, it created a greater market for fresh produce and in effect mandated a year-long growing season in California—and thereby a much greater need for its cars. By 1943 PFE had 40,800 refrigerator cars, and these had substantially more capacity than the early reefers.

In its heyday, PFE loaded dozens of trains daily on both the UP and SP all over California and Oregon. They were forwarded east in long dedicated trains—known to railroaders as "Fruit Blocks"—over all three of UP's primary arteries: the Los Angeles & Salt Lake, the Overland Route (via SP), and the Oregon lines. While perishable traffic moved year round, the pattern ebbed and flowed cyclically in response to harvest seasons. Typically there were several peak rushes during the course of the year. At these times it was crucial to have cars ready to handle ripe or near-ripe produce, otherwise the produce could be lost rotting in the fields while waiting for transport. Such an event would be ruinous to both farmers and PFE. In peak fruit season in the heyday of the Fruit Block, SP might deliver as many as seven trains a day to the UP at Ogden. Yet in quieter times, traffic would be much less, and a block of reefers coming over SP might be combined with reefers off the LA&SL at Ogden before continuing east.

Even with fast expedited scheduling, it typically it took a week for a perishable train loaded in Northern California to reach Chicago. In the days before mechanically cooled refrigerator cars, Fruit Blocks required special service stops so that reefers could be restocked with ice to maintain a cool temperature. Icing was accomplished quickly and efficiently using huge icing facilities that were maintained by PFE at strategic locations. Pacific Fruit Express operated 18 such plants on UP and SP lines, the largest of which was at SP's Roseville Yard near Sacramento where many Fruit Blocks destined to travel across the Overland Route were assembled. This gigantic facility could accommodate as many as 254 reefers at one time. PFE icing facilities on UP lines were situated at Ogden, Laramie, Cheyenne, North Platte, and Council Bluffs, among other places. Icing was accomplished amazingly fast, and typically just a minute was allowed to ice each car. Maury Klein reports in his book, *Union Pacific: the Rebirth*, that, in 1927, PFE's North Platte plant could provide ice for up to 1,000 cars a day. Ice blocks weighing several tons were loaded into hatches at either end of the car while melted icewater was drained off. In order to keep produce moving expeditiously, an eastbound perishable train would only pause for ice where necessary, although the number of such stops varied with the rate that the ice was melting. A train's speed over the railroad together with prevailing outside temperatures had a great effect on the frequency of icing stops. Regular checks were made as a train moved east to determine where and when it needed to stop. In addition, since produce could also be damaged by frost, it was important that, in the winter, reefers did not get too cold; heaters were sometimes applied to keep produce from freezing.

One of the most interesting services offered to perishable shippers was the ability to alter the destination of a loaded car as it made its way east. Shippers were permitted to change the final destination of a car up to four times without additional charges. This allowed them to direct their goods toward the most suitable market as demand fluctuated during the trip east. What may seem especially amazing by today's standards was that these complicated route changes were effected long before computers, fax machines, and cellular telephones played a role in railroad operations.

Trains originating at Roseville were given an "RV" symbol, while those coming from Colton, California, would use a "CN" symbol. The 40-foot length of reefers remained standard, although the carrying capacity of the cars gradually increased, resulting in heavier and heavier trains. A typical 1940s-era insulated car weighed 26 tons empty and accommodated up to 32 tons of produce. Where in the 1920s trains could operate as long as 80 cars, the heavier cars of the late steam era resulted in much heavier trains, and by the 1940s Union Pacific generally limited Fruit Blocks to a maximum of either 70 cars or 3,200 tons east of Ogden. By today's standards, 3,200 tons is comparatively light—UP now runs trains almost five times as heavy—but at that time this was considered heavy for a boxcar train, and it was the limit that UP's most powerful locomotives could handle over the mountains. Over the Wasatch Mountains, heavy Fruit Blocks were usually hauled by 4-8-8-4 Big Boys and on the less-demanding territory east of Green River by 4-6-6-4 Challengers. UP used its three-cylinder 4-12-2 "Union Pacific" types for Fruit Blocks east of North Platte. Fruit Blocks were resorted at Laramie, North Platte, and Council Bluffs. North Platte was the dividing point for traffic destined east to Omaha or to Kansas City. At these two cities, perishable trains were broken up and their cars distributed to UP's various eastward connections. During lulls, it was not uncommon to "fill" a Fruit Block with general traffic east of North Platte.

The advent of the government-sponsored Interstate highway decimated PFE's traffic during the 1960s and 1970s. While as many as three daily trains were still being handed over by the SP to the UP at Ogden during that period, by the early 1980s this traffic had almost entirely vanished. Icing facilities had been rendered redundant by the advent of the mechanical reefer, and the need for a jointly owned company to operate and maintain reefers was deemed no longer necessary. In 1978 PFE was split up and became Union Pacific Fruit Express and Southern Pacific Fruit Express. Today some perishable traffic still moves across the Overland Route in reefers, but it is trickle compared to what it had been. Most

perishable traffic is now carried in truck trailers, however some of these still move by rail on TOFC trains.

LIVESTOCK TRAINS

The western plains of Wyoming, Idaho, and Montana is big sky and cowboy country—where cattle graze on open grange, and sheep and pigs are raised by the tens of thousands. This is the meat that feeds America: hamburgers on four legs and pork chops rolling in the mud. Animals are raised in the open country and then given a one-way ticket to the cities for slaughter, packaging, and distribution.

Union Pacific has a long history bringing livestock to market. Traditionally, animals raised in the West would travel eastward to slaughter houses in Kansas City, Omaha, and Chicago. Chicago's stockyards, once located south of downtown, were made famous by Upton Sinclair's sensationalist novel *The Jungle*, which dramatized the evils of the meat-packing industry. However as the population of the Western U.S. grew, the market for meat grew proportionately and shifted from east to west. For many years California was the fastest-growing region of the nation. By the 1930s the flow of livestock reversed from an eastward bias to a westward flow.

By the advent of World War II, Union Pacific was handling an enormous volume of livestock traffic westward over its LA&SL line to the Los Angeles Union Stock yards. At this time, livestock trains typically took 56 hours or more to make the 790-mile run across the Utah, Nevada, and Southern California deserts

One of UP's famous Fruit Blocks—a solid train of refrigerator cars carrying perishables out of the West Coast—storms along the Overland Route main line at Emory, Utah, during World War II. This was Union Pacific in its finest hour, an integral part of the massive war effort. The 4-8-8-4 Big Boys often assigned to these high-priority trains could move these heavy trains at high speed over sawtooth terrain. *Union Pacific Museum Collection, image No. SFA-50* to Los Angeles. In the steam era this was a slow, arduous journey, and livestock trains, like most through freights, plodded along behind 2-10-2s and other ponderous locomotive types. The LA&SL is a brutal mountain railroad with some of the toughest, longest grades in the U.S., and its multiple summits required a host complex helper arrangements. Its primarily single-track main line made for complicated operations that could strain the patience of even experienced dispatchers. Furthermore, locomotives needed to pause for fuel and water on a regular basis, and although livestock runs had a high priority, they still had to get "in the clear" (out of the way) for the crack *Los Angeles Limited*, *Challenger,* or the flashy *City of Los Angeles* streamliner. The best a livestock run could hope was to move at an average speed of just 14 to 15 mph. This slow rate further delayed the run because of federal regulations mandated for livestock moves. For the health of the animals, the law required that they were to be taken off the trains at least once every 28 hours for food, water, and rest. At the option of the livestock owner, this limit could be extended by a maximum of eight additional hours, but not a minute longer. All animals were refreshed at Salt Lake City before departing for Los Angeles and were refreshed again in Las Vegas.

Although its livestock trade was booming, UP was beginning to feel competition from highway traffic and, following World War II, made a serious effort to improve its livestock operations. In the late 1940s, threefold improvements facilitated significantly faster livestock moves and secured UP's hold on the business for another decade. During the war, Union Pacific had installed Centralized Traffic Control over Cima Hill west of Las Vegas, an improvement that dramatically eased operations on this tough piece of desert railroad. Following the war, UP expanded CTC over most of its LA&SL route, smoothing operations and expanding capacity. The second major operational improvement was the complete dieselization of mainline operations on the LA&SL using brand-new Electro-Motive F3 and Alco FA diesels. The heavy demands of this route, combined with poor water and remote operations, made the line a prime candidate for diesels. UP rebuilt 800 of its stockcars and equipped them with Timken roller bearings between 1947 and 1948. This dramatically reduced both the amount of maintenance required and the chance of a hot box, which could delay or, worse, derail a train. In 1947 UP cut the time of its Salt Lake City–Los Angeles run from 32 to just 27 hours. By shortening the time, UP eliminated the

The post-World War II boom in the trucking industry resulted in most U.S. railroads losing much of their perishable traffic. Nonetheless, some perishables still do move by rail. Sparkling in the Wyoming sunset, an eastbound with a block of vegetable-laden reefers on the head end howls through Hermosa in 1993. *John Leopard*

mandatory rest stop at Las Vegas, a move that dramatically cut operating costs while providing better service. By the 1950s, livestock moves running from Omaha to Los Angeles would routinely take just five days.

Stock cars were loaded at various points in Wyoming, Idaho, and Montana and then routed to Salt Lake City where they were assembled into *Stock Special*s (later known as the *Day Live Stock* or *DLS*) and expedited to Los Angeles. In the late 1940s and early 1950s this service was characterized by a quartet of shiny yellow bulldog-nose Electro-Motive F3s hauling a matched consist of 65–75 Armour yellow stockcars. These were handsome trains and the subject of UP publicity photos of the era.

During the 1950s, Union Pacific modernized its Cheyenne stockyards to improve handling and speed the feeding and watering of animals. Well-known railroad author of the period, S. Kip Farrington Jr., described the new facility in detail, noting that it had 20 percent more capacity than the one it had replaced. Little did UP know at the time that its livestock trade would soon decline. In his book, *Union Pacific's Salt Lake Route*, Mark Hemphill explains that although livestock business boomed during 1950s, it soon declined and that by the 1990s only a handful of stockcars were traveling over the LA&SL route, usually for a single customer in L.A. By the 1990s, livestock business had completely vanished from

most other railroads, making UP's runs among the very last regular livestock moves in the U.S. an anomaly on a modern railroad.

INTERMODAL

Intermodal operations began inauspiciously in 1953 as an experimental TOFC service between Los Angeles and Las Vegas. The service was enormously successful and has become one of Union Pacific's largest sources of traffic. Within five years of the first intermodal runs, UP was operating TOFC trains over 2,500 route-miles, roughly 25 percent of its whole system. It had acquired 145 piggyback flats and 216 highway trailers. At that time the railroad was proud that it was moving 12 trailers a day through Los Angeles. This volume would skyrocket during the years to come, and by 1994, following the advent of double-stack technology, UP was carrying more than 330,000 intermodal shipments via Los Angeles every year. Today the container-hauling steamship company APL Limited (the successor to American President Lines) is UP's largest customer, and UP is one of the largest intermodal carriers in North America.

COAL

Coal has played an important role in UP operations since the railroad began. Thomas Durant lobbied for an amendment to the Pacific Rail Act of 1862 to allow the railroad

The railroad industry was particularly vulnerable to the loss of livestock traffic to truckers after World War II. Yet, UP managed to hang on to some livestock traffic much later than other carriers. Chasing the setting sun, a westbound *California Livestock Special* at Dale Junction, Wyoming, in July 1970 has a block of steel stockcars at the head end, with general freight filling out the rest of the train. *Steve Smedley*

mineral rights on its Federal land grants, specifically to take advantage of coal reserves his geologists had located along the railroad's proposed right-of-way through the Medicine Bow region of central Wyoming. Union Pacific's first coal mine was located by General Dodge near Brownes Pass in the Saddleback Hills. At first, UP mined coal in Wyoming to supply fuel for its locomotives and those of the Central Pacific, but it also delivered coal to communities along its line. The coal business proved especially lucrative, and by the mid 1870s UP operated seven coal mines in Wyoming, located at Carbon, Evanston, and Rock Springs. UP's coal mines flourished under the direction of business mogul Jay Gould. While Gould had his hands in many businesses at that time, UP's coal appears to have been one his favorites. Author Maury Klein reports that Gould admitted in 1876, "You know, this coal business is a sort of hobby of mine." That year UP hauled roughly 265,000 tons of coal. Gould was very successful with his "hobby," and by 1883 UP moved more than 900,000 tons of coal.

Union Pacific developed coal mines in Colorado and Utah as well as Wyoming. One of the principal coal-hauling routes has been its Los Angeles & Salt Lake route which handled coal traffic interchanged from both the Rio Grande and the Utah Railway at Provo in addition to Wyoming coal. Although some coal is burned for electric power in Southern California, it is shipped over the LA&SL for a variety purposes. Mark Hemphill, who details LA&SL coal moves, explains that in 1942 the UP began moving coal to the Kaiser Steel Mill in Fontana, California, and in the mid 1960s the railroad began handling export coal to the Far East shipped from Los Angeles. He notes that by 1994, an estimated 10 million tons of Colorado and Utah coal were rolling west over the LA&SL.

This figure is a mere trickle compared to UP's largest coal source, Wyoming's Powder River Basin. In the scope of Union Pacific operations, Powder River coal is one of its newest sources of traffic—and also one of its largest. Initially UP reached the Powder River via Chicago & North Western's lines to South Dakota, Wyoming, and Nebraska. The first C&NW coal train left the Powder River on August 16, 1984. The business gradually swelled, so by the time UP merged the C&NW in 1995, as many as 30 coal trains were loaded in the Powder River Basin every day—86.7 million tons of coal a year. When C&NW served the Powder River, coal trains were interchanged with the Union Pacific at South Morrill, Nebraska, and often ran through over UP rails with C&NW locomotives. Today it is one seamless operation.

In 1999 Union Pacific boasted that it was moving more than 130 million tons of coal a year systemwide, or an average of 356,000 tons of coal a day—significantly more than the railroad moved all year in 1876! Gould would have been astonished at this incredible volume, but likely proud of the high figure.

IRON ORE

In the vast scope of Union Pacific's freight operations, its iron ore moves may seem just a bit trifle, yet UP has been a major ore carrier for many years. Over the years the railroad has carried iron ore from a variety of locations—both on line and from interchange—to steel-producing plants in the Salt Lake City/Provo area, to Kaiser Steel in California, and for export via Long Beach, California. In 1957, UP carried nearly 73,000 carloads of ore, or roughly 200 loads, every day. Traditionally most of UP's ore was mined and consumed in Utah; the Iron Mountain mine was located near Lund on the Cedar City branch. Most of the ore from this mine was destined for smelters in Provo. Other Utah iron mines were located at Iron Springs, Comstock, and Desert Mound. Some ore was mined at Butte, Montana, and carried over Monida Pass to Salt Lake City.

Union Pacific's contemporary ore movements primarily involve taconite that is mined and pelletized on the Duluth, Missabe & Iron Range in northern Minnesota and then transported by way of the Overland Route to Geneva Steel in Utah. UP handles an average of three of these trains daily including empty moves. In 1994 Union Pacific temporarily lost this business to a Wisconsin Central-Southern Pacific routing but regained it after the merger with SP in 1996.

UNION PACIFIC YARDS

UP's freight yards and terminals have grown enormously as business has steadily expanded, and especially so in the post-World War II environment. Explosive growth of California and the West combined with general economic prosperity in the U.S. has made the UP a primary freight corridor. However, the nature of its yards has evolved over the years as traffic has shifted from conventional boxcar trains to intermodal moves and unit commodity trains.

At one time Union Pacific had extensive facilities for its perishable traffic and livestock moves, but with the loss of this traditional traffic these facilities have been abandoned or converted for other purposes. In the last 40

A rolling skyscraper of stacked containers, an American President Lines (APL) train sweeps eastward through Oxman, Oregon, in 1993. *Brian Solomon*

years, the UP has made a large investment in intermodal yards and transfer points to meet modern traffic demands. Its booming coal business and automobile traffic also requires new, specialized facilities. Yet, UP's general freight remains big business and requires vast yards for switching and sorting cars.

North Platte

Union Pacific's sprawling Bailey Yard at North Platte is not only the largest, most important yard on the railroad, but as of 1994 Bailey is the largest classification yard in the world. It is named for past UP president Edd Bailey. Located 281 miles west of Omaha, North Platte is strategically situated at the operational center of the traditional (pre mega-merger) Union Pacific. Traffic moving through the Omaha/Council Bluffs and Kansas City gateways can be processed for shipment to all West Coast points on the traditional UP system. West of North Platte, freight moved to Denver via Julesburg or Cheyenne; to Pacific Northwest points via Granger, Wyoming; to Northern California via the Ogden/Salt Lake City gateway; and to Los Angeles and Southern California via the LA&SL route.

UP invested hundreds of millions of dollars in its infrastructure after World War II. Among its significant improvements was the construction of a massive new yard, five miles long, at North Platte, which was opened in November 1948. This facility included four primary sections, including a 1,400-car hump yard, a 1,200-car receiving yard, and a 1,600-car departure yard. During the mid-1950s, UP modernized its North Platte classification facilities by introducing a computer controlled "push-button" hump. By employing electronically controlled retarders, UP expanded hump capacity and reduced the number of damaged loads caused by hard coupling. The computer gauges the speed of cars descending the hump by inputs from infrared sensors and regulates speed through the control of retarders that mechanically grip the wheels.

Between 1966 and 1970, UP expanded its North Platte Yard and renamed it Bailey Yard. A second hump was constructed for eastbound traffic while the original 1948 hump was designated for westbound traffic. A new diesel shop was opened in 1971. Traffic continued to grow, and in 1980 UP opened an expanded westbound hump. In 1984 UP began handling Powder River Coal through Bailey. This traffic joins the main line a few miles west of North Platte at O'Fallons, Nebraska. Coal business boomed in the late 1980s and 1990s, and UP built a huge coal-train marshalling yard at North Platte to accommodate the growing parade of coal trains. This facility can store up to 450 coal hoppers on seven specially designated tracks.

In 1999, Bailey Yard has become the dominant feature of North Platte—the yard occupies 2,850 acres, and stretches over eight miles of main line. Union Pacific boasts that the yard handles an average of 10,000 cars daily, and every day its twin humps sort an average of

Railroads have always done particularly well hauling bulk commodities, and UP is no exception. When the mining of the low-sulphur coal in Wyoming's Powder River Basin took off early in the 1980s, it created a traffic boom for the UP (and the C&NW when it was independent) that lasts to this day. Sunset's golden glow christens an eastbound Powder River coal train near Dixon, Illinois, in late fall 1999. *Dan Montague*

3,000 cars. The two hump yards alone account for 114 tracks, and the whole yard is comprised of 315 miles of track—more track than found on most American shortline railroads. The parade of trains is equally impressive. On average, UP handles 135 trains through North Platte daily, including 64 coal trains and coal empties. While congestion occasionally causes traffic to back up at the yard, UP claims its average car terminal time through the yard to be just 11 hours and 30 minutes.

The yard's immense size and the vast number of heavy freight trains through it everyday have made Bailey somewhat of a tourist attraction. It attracts thousands of visitors every year to watch trains, and as a result, UP has built a small visitors' center on the south side of the yard near the locomotive shops.

UP advertises Bailey as "the world's leading railroad yard" and an "economic barometer for America." It is the railroad's showcase facility and source of great company pride.

Utah Yards

Ogden was the traditional terminal of the UP's end of the Overland Route. Here, UP transferred passengers and interchanged freight with the Central Pacific (later Southern Pacific). As a result, UP's yards in the area have long played an important role in operations. Today, Ogden's yards play a less important position in UP freight operations as there is no longer need to interchange traffic with SP now

that it is part of the UP, yet Ogden still serves a variety of local customers.

Salt Lake City's North Yard has remained a vital, important facility on the railroad. In 1994 it had a 17-track flat (non-hump) classification yard and 12-track receiving and departure yard. It originated and terminated an average of seven trains daily while sorting an average of 900 cars. In addition, it had an intermodal facility that handled an average of 264 containers a day.

California Yards

Unlike Santa Fe and SP, Union Pacific traditionally did not operate a vast network of branch lines in California. Most of its California traffic was generated in the Los Angeles Basin including port traffic from both Los Angeles and Long Beach. The 1982 purchase of Western Pacific provided UP with access to Northern California, and UP's California access and market share was further improved with its acquisition of the SP in 1996.

East Yard in Los Angeles was UP's primary California facility for many years. Mark Hemphill reports in his *Union Pacific's Salt Lake Route* that in 1924–25 the LA&SL constructed a major facility at East Yard consisting of a 1,000-car receiving yard, a 700-car eastbound classification yard, an 880-car westbound classification yard, and a significant locomotive shop. During the World War II traffic boom, UP expanded the capacity of the

Hump engine SD38–2R No. 2820 at Houston's Englewood Yard takes a break on the inbound track as another cut of cars gets shoved over the hump during the late afternoon of March 21, 1998. Englewood was inherited from the Southern Pacific, and, shortly after the UP-SP merger, congestion at the facility prompted the Surface Transportation Board to put the Port Terminal Railway on alert to assume yard operations at this critical hub. *Tom Kline* crucial facility. In the early 1970s, UP built a 16-track hump yard here, but as the role of intermodal traffic became increasingly important, UP converted large portions of the yard to intermodal operation. The hump was shut down in 1990, and the yard became primarily an intermodal terminal. In 1994, East Yard had just 12 tracks for general traffic, with seven tracks for intermodal work.

Adjacent to East Yard is Weeds Yard used for industrial switching. Prior to the merger with SP, which greatly expanded UP's Los Angeles terminal capacity, UP also operated several smaller support yards in the L.A. Basin. It had a nine-track local yard at City of Industry, a seven-track facility at Montclair, and a three-track yard a Mira Loma.

Land is inexpensive in the desert compared to the high price of real estate in L.A., which is why during 1980 and 1981 UP built a new 24-track, 1,500-car yard in the Mojave Desert at Yermo, California, east of Daggett where UP's LA&SL route joins the Santa Fe. This yard was built to handle merchandise traffic so that UP could convert its Los Angeles facility to an intermodal hub without expanding the size of the yard. Yermo has been further expanded to handle growing traffic, and by 1994 it consisted of an 8-track receiving/departure yard, a 19-track flat switching classification yard, plus an older 7-track yard, a car shop, and locomotive servicing shop.

Oregon Yards

Union Pacific's largest yard in the Pacific Northwest is its massive facility at Hinkle, Oregon, which classifies traffic from all over western Oregon and Washington state. It is located on the main line west of the Blue Mountains. In 1996 Union Pacific expanded Hinkle's locomotive shop so that it can service 90 locomotives every day.

Portland has long served as the UP's principal terminal in the Northwest, and UP has maintained several yards there. Its two primary facilities in the years prior to the SP merger were Albina and Barnes yards. Albina had a 5-track receiving and departure yard, a 24-car classification yard, a 7-track local facility, and an intermodal terminal. In 1994, Albina processed an average of 1,200 cars a day

Barnes Yard served a host of industries in the port area, plus two large grain elevators and an auto-unloading facility. It had 22 tracks and hosted an average of 15 yard and local freights daily. Union Pacific also maintained

several satellite facilities in the Portland area, including Rivergate Yard, Bonneville Yard, and Kenton Yard. Following the its merger with SP, UP inherited SP's Brooklyn Yard which primarily had served as an intermodal facility in recent years.

UP operated smaller yards at traditional division points and junctions with branch lines. For example, La Grande, Oregon, was the location of the junction with the Joseph branch and a base for helpers used on the Blue Mountain and Burnt Mountain grades. Farther east, UP once operated a decent-size facility at Huntington, Oregon, the traditional meeting point of Oregon Short Line and the Oregon Railway & Navigation Company.

Idaho Yards

Idaho is one of those states often overlooked in railroad operations, however Union Pacific has had a considerable presence in this state over the years. Its primary yard is at Pocatello where the main line from Granger to Portland intersects the Salt Lake City–Butte route. This had long been an important yard facility, and in the late 1940s UP built a large modern facility here that included a retarder hump and a major car shop. UP's hump featured a 4 percent grade that sent cars rolling into a 28-track classification yard. In addition there was a 14-track receiving yard and an 11-track departure yard. The modern facility was capable of accommodating 2,200 cars daily on the eve of the Korean War, and UP processed a great variety of traffic here ranging from perishable goods and livestock to bulk minerals, lumber, and mixed freight.

HELPER DISTRICTS

Union Pacific may not be the first traditional Western railroad that comes to mind when helper operations are considered, but the railroad has its share of tough grades and consequentially a long history of helper operations. Sherman Hill is mild compared to the likes of SP's Donner Pass or Rio Grande's Tennessee Pass, yet it required helpers in steam days. Likewise, heavy trains working east from Ogden up through Weber and Echo canyons needed assistance in the days before diesels. Although these rises on the Wyoming Division warranted attention from managers, the far more severe grades are located to the west.

The Los Angeles & Salt Lake Route features a brutal sawtooth profile that challenged the locomotive operators in steam days. Crestline

and Cima Hills represent some of the longest sustained grades in the U.S. Fortunately, the toughest pulls are eastbound, and since the prevailing flow of traffic on UP is westbound, the difficulties have been minimized. Cima Hill features a 2.2 percent grade eastbound and just a 1 percent grade westbound.

Located east of Las Vegas, the town of Caliente, Nevada, was a junction, a division point, and also the helper base for Crestline Hill back in steam days. The grade stiffened west of the helper terminal, and steam helpers would run west from Caliente to Leith, in the Meadow Valley Wash, to meet eastbound freights. After tying on, they would assist them up through Caliente and along Clover Creek Canyon to Crestline. Some heavy trains would require a second helper which was usually added at Caliente. Occasionally, heavy westbound trains would also need help, and they were assisted with a Caliente-based helper from Modena to Crestline. Likewise, Kelso, California—located west of Las Vegas—was the helper base for Cima Hill.

When diesels came in the late 1940s, it spelled an end for helpers on most trains between Daggett, California, and Milford, Utah. This was one of the big selling points for dieselization on the LA&SL and why UP focused its early freight diesels here while other lines retained steam for another dozen years. In the 1980s, helpers were reintroduced to the LA&SL when long, heavy double-stack trains began operating east from Los Angeles. On these trains, through helpers were used over both Cima and Crestline Hills.

The most serious grade on the LA&SL is between Victorville and San Bernardino over Cajon Pass on the line owned by the Santa Fe. This was serious obstacle in steam days, often requiring multiple helpers, particularly on the grueling east slope. It is still a challenging climb that requires helpers on most heavy freights. In steam days, 2-10-2s ruled as helpers, although some 4-10-2s also worked over Cajon. At the end of steam, these were supplanted by Fairbanks-Morse H20-44s and Electro Motive TR5 cow-and-calf sets. Interestingly, both of these locomotive types were delivered without multiple-unit controls, which mandated an engineer in each locomotive if more than one helper unit was required. In modern times, pairs of SD40–2s have been typical Cajon helpers.

One of the toughest main lines on the traditional UP is the route between Granger and Portland which features a number of difficult climbs that still require helpers in the diesel era. There are three summits in northeastern Oregon between Huntington and Hinkle. The first is Encina Hill, followed by Telocasset Hill, and then the big climb over the Blue Mountains to the summit at Kamela. In modern times, helpers have been based at La Grange, Oregon, located at the base of the east slope of the Blue Mountains, to work east or west as needed. The steep grades, often exceeding 2 percent, frequently require helpers both ascending and descending—the latter to assist with braking. In the mid-1990s this was one of the first places UP implemented distributed power units (see chapter 7), operated by radio remote control. East of Boise, Idaho, the 1.55 percent westbound grade climbing out of the Snake River Valley from Glens Ferry to Reverse also warrants helper operations on heavy trains.

It's 1 A.M. at North Platte but floodlights provide plenty of illumination at UP's Bailey Yard while locomotives—including a Centennial—get serviced prior to their next assignment. Bailey serves as the heart of UP freight operations. The mammoth facility was heavily upgraded beginning in the mid-1960s, and on October 25, 1968, was dedicated by UP Chairman Frank E. Barnett in honor of Edd H. Bailey, then UP president. *Steve Smedley*

For over a century, Union Pacific moved passengers over its system, initially in crude wooden cars and finally in luxurious streamlined equipment on a fleet of streamlined trains. Hundreds of UP employees, from conductors to ticket agents to car attendants, acted as the railroad's ambassadors, such as this affable car attendant at the ready for passengers boarding the final *City of Los Angeles* at Las Vegas, Nevada, on May 2, 1971—the very last day of UP passenger service. *Jim Heuer*

Riding the Rails of Union Pacific

THE COLORFUL HISTORY OF UP PASSENGER SERVICE

Transcontinental travelers today have little appreciation for the vast distance between east and west. Whether they are soaring at 36,000 feet in a Boeing or racing along on I-80 in a Ford, the time it takes to go from coast to coast is just a fraction of what it was just 150 years ago.

It was the railroad that slashed the transcontinental travel time from months to just a few days. Yet, the early trains, while they made a trip west faster, did not take away from the wonder and aura of a journey across the great American West. In its early years, Union Pacific passenger trains were more than just a way west; they had become for all practical purposes *the* way west. By today's standards of comfort and speed, those early trains seem primitive and painfully slow. The equipment was crude and crowded, the fares were high, and yet the railroad represented such a vast improvement in transcontinental travel that complaints were relatively few.

In 1884, Frederick E. Shearer compiled *The Pacific Tourist*, an early guidebook aimed at Western travelers. Today it reveals the excitement and adventure anticipated by travelers headed into a West that offered unequaled sights, untold tales, and unlimited opportunity. So, while the thought of a week-long journey, suffering in the confines of a bouncy, non-air-conditioned, wooden railway car without the opportunity to shower, enjoy a decent meal, or even an uninterrupted night's sleep now seems like torture, it was then considered the epitome of luxurious modern travel. The train was a vehicle of optimism and hope, and the exuberance of the railway passenger could overcome all the hardships and discomforts of early railway travel.

Shearer paints this early railway journey in the kindest language. After just a few paragraphs, the right-thinking modern reader may wish that those early trains still ran, and a ride on the UP was still the best way west:

> "At Council Bluffs or Kansas City, as you view the long train just ready to leave the depot for its overland trip, the appearance of strength, massiveness, and majestic power you will admit to be exceedingly beautiful and impressive; this feeling is still more intensified when a day or so later, alone out upon the upland plains, you stand at a little distance and look down the long train, the handsomest work of science ever made for the comfort of earth's travelers."

He continues,

> "A Pullman Palace car in motion is a grand and beautiful sight too, from within as well as without. On some lovely, balmy, summer day when the fresh breeze across the prairies induce us to open our doors and windows, there may often been seen curious and pleasant sights. Standing at the rear of the train, and with all the doors open, there is an unobstructed view along the aisles throughout the entire length. On either side of the train are the prairies, where the eye sees but wilderness and even desolation, then looking back upon this long aisle or avenue, he sees civilization and comfort and luxury. How sharp the contrast."

His words reveal the exhilarating adventure of rail travel to the West that is lost upon most contemporary travelers, regardless of their mode of transport.

OVERLAND ROUTE TRAINS

Initially, service across the Union Pacific for California was provided by a train referred to simply as the *Express*, later the *Pacific Express*. Westbound this train brought passengers within sight of its namesake ocean, but its similarly named eastbound counterpart, the *Atlantic Express*, fell far short of its name by several hundred miles. After 1906, the westbound train acquired an even more-ambitious name, *China & Japan Express.*

Trains operating to and from Chicago were handled by Chicago & North Western east of Omaha. C&NW would even supply cars for selected trains as part of the arrangement of through operations.

As time went on, the trains were improved. Realizing that there was money to be had in catering to the upper-echelon traveler, UP in the last quarter of the nineteenth

914   GREAT SALT LAKE CUT-OFF AT SUNSET, GREAT SALT LAKE, UTAH

3A-H214

The Overland Limited *was one of the earliest flagship trains of the Overland Route between Chicago and San Francisco Bay. Jointly operated by the Chicago & North Western, UP, and Southern Pacific, a heavyweight-era* Overland *is shown in a colorized postcard from the 1920s heading over the Great Salt Lake on SP's Lucin Cutoff. Dave Oroszi collection*

century experimented with a variety of deluxe services. The *Golden Gate Special* debuted between Council Bluffs and the Bay Area in December 1888. This was no small affair, with UP and Central Pacific promoting the run as the "The Finest Train in the World." This fancy train exuded the style of the times, employing plush, ornately decorated cars. There was only enough equipment for one train, thus it made just one round trip per week. UP apparently misjudged the potential of such a opulent run, for the train failed after less than a year. In 1889, the slightly less opulent *Overland Flyer*, a train that had begun running in 1887, assumed the *Golden Gate Special*'s services.

The famed *Overland Limited* began service in 1896 and quickly earned its place in American passenger-train lore. The train's official name varied over the years, listed in the

timetables as *Overland Limited, San Francisco Overland Limited*, and the *San Francisco Overland*, but it was simply the *Overland* to most passengers. This train was known for its luxurious accommodations, consistently good service, and modern amenities.

Harriman control brought about numerous improvements to UP's premier train. He upgraded its route with better track, time-saving line relocations, and automatic block signals for safety. Running times were tightened significantly. Prior to Harriman control of the UP, a passenger train typically took 73 hours to make the run from Chicago to the West Coast. His initial improvements shaved 10 hours from the schedule, but by the 1920s additional upgrades allowed the *Overland Limited* to make the run in just 58 hours.

Harriman upgraded the *Overland* itself. In 1902 the train was re-equipped with new, state-of-the-art, steel-framed cars, making it one of the first trains in America to use such equipment. There were other wonders too. The train was also equipped with that modern communication innovation, the telephone—a marvel to behold in an era when the railroad was still run with a primitive telegraph communication system, and only the very rich could afford telephones in their homes.

Phones were nice, but food was important too, and one of the *Overland*'s shining stars was its dining car, the *Manhattan*, a steel-framed, wooden-sheathed gem of a diner. A Pullman product of 1900, the *Manhattan* featured fully enclosed vestibules—another new improvement in rail passenger technology. Enclosed vestibules (passageways between cars) added an element of safety and comfort by enabling passengers to pass between cars without being exposed to the elements. Among the car's elegant accessories were electric lights—then considered an extravagance—instead of gas lamps.

With the luxurious treatment offered by the *Overland*, the railroad would soon spoil travelers into thinking that drafty, dark, uncomfortable passenger cars were not an acceptable mode of modern travel. Yet, the railroad continued to improve the service over the years.

After World War II, the *Overland* truly performed a transcontinental service as it carried through sleepers for both New York City and Washington, D.C. In 1951 the train was given new, streamlined rolling stock. It soldiered on—right into a decade that would witness a severe downward spiral in rail passenger service. Despite its luxurious accommodations and long track record, this elder statesman of Union Pacific passenger trains had finally outlived its usefulness and in 1962 was in essence discontinued when it was combined with the *City of San Francisco*.

UP knew there was nothing like a little excitement to attract riders to the rails. Under the influence of a robust economy, UP and Chicago & North Western let a new flower bloom in 1927 when they debuted the *Columbine*, a classy train connecting Chicago and Denver. Named for Colorado's state flower, the *Columbine* carried an open-platform observation car sporting a bold drumhead displaying the popular blossom. In a public celebration on May 15, 1927, the governor of Colorado christened the new train.

The *Columbine* wasn't the only blossom in UP's fleet, and for many years the premier train to Oregon was UP's *Portland Rose*. It linked Chicago and Portland, with a connection service to Tacoma and Seattle. Connecting service was also available from Kansas City via Denver, with through coaches and sleepers from Denver to Portland and to Spokane.

UP's "Jack of all trains" was the *Pacific Limited.* The train linked Chicago with Portland, San Francisco, and Los Angeles, and there was a section from Kansas City and Denver connecting at Cheyenne. It was really several trains, carrying the numbers 21, 23, 25 westbound and 22, 24, 26 eastbound. All ran combined as a single train for the trip across Illinois, Iowa, Nebraska, and part of Wyoming.

Unlike UP's better-known transcontinental trains, the *Pacific Limited* made numerous local stops. For example, the train made as many as 40 station stops across Nebraska's heartland. If you lived in small-town America, this is the train you would have chosen to ride west—those fancier limiteds didn't always stop in your town.

UP DEBUTS THE STREAMLINED TRAIN

The combined effects of the automobile and the Great Depression of the 1930s caused UP's passenger ridership to plummet. By 1932, passenger loads were only 23.6 percent of the number that had carried in 1920. UP embarked on a radical plan that would attract passengers back to the rails while reducing operational costs.

UP decided that the conventional passenger train was no longer good enough. Trains of

Another steam-era passenger-train scene on the Union Pacific shows 4-6-2 No. 2897 on secondary run at an unknown location circa 1930. The open-platform business car sandwiched by the engine and Railway Post Office car appears to be deadheading (being transferred without occupants). *Otto C. Perry, Denver Public Library, Western History Department*

McKeen's Windsplitters

At the turn of the century, the high cost of branchline passenger trains was troubling the Union Pacific, so it searched for a better, cheaper means of serving its branchline customers. A novel solution, while not entirely original, typified Union Pacific's independent pioneering approach toward motive power and problem-solving.

In the late 1890s, emerging internal-combustion technology appeared to offer an alternative to steam power. Several companies in England and America constructed gasoline-powered railway cars for commercial purposes with marginal success. In 1904, UP's E. H. Harriman asked UP's motive power chief, William J. McKeen, to develop a practical railcar suitable for passenger service on the UP. McKeen, working with UP engineers, took on the task with zeal and set out to build a fast, efficient railway vehicle that out-performed both earlier internal-combustion-powered cars and conventional steam trains. He had studied wind-resistant principles revealed by the famous Berlin-Zossen high-speed propulsion tests and similar experiments conducted just after the turn of the century. He was keenly aware that, while wind resistance is insignificant at slower speeds, it has serious effect on performance at high speeds.

In March 1905, McKeen designed and built a prototype with a wind-resistance profile that featured a knife-like prow, a rounded rear end, and a semi-streamlined body with minimal protrusions. His first car, No. M-1 ("M" for motor), was constructed at UP's Omaha Shops. It was 31 feet long, rode on a single two-axle truck with 42-inch wheels, and powered by a vertical, six-cylinder Riotte gasoline engine that developed 100 hp. One of the significant differences between McKeen's rail car and most other American railcars was the use of a mechanical transmission instead of an electric transmission as later applied to popular gas-electric cars.

After initial testing in Omaha and Salt Lake City, Harriman had the prototype sent to Portland where anti-smoke regulations threatened to hamper his railroad's operations. The prototype experienced some serious difficulties, but McKeen, undaunted by its failings, refined his designs and constructed a second car. This one was 55 feet long and featured two trucks, setting the precedent for later McKeen cars.

Although the cars had their foibles, Harriman seemed pleased with McKeen's creations, and in 1908 he provided McKeen with resources to set up the McKeen Railcar Company. With this backing, McKeen resigned his position at UP and went into business building railcars full time for Harriman and other customers.

The typical McKeen car featured a 70-foot-long, all-steel body with McKeen's signature knife-edge nose and a rounded rear, a tapered roof, and rows of distinctive porthole windows on the sides. His later cars weighed between 34 and 40 tons and were powered by 200-hp gasoline engines that McKeen and his engineers had adapted from a marine engine design. McKeen's cars were popularly known as "Windsplitters," but there is certain irony in this description: It turns out that McKeen had the fundamentals of wind-resistant design backwards. The tear-drop shape that he employed works most effectively when the rounded end leads, as demonstrated by most modern aircraft designs. Furthermore, although McKeen had noble intentions of building high-speed cars, they were typically assigned to branch lines and rarely ran faster than 50 mph. At such slow speeds the advantages of an air-resistant design are negligible.

For a short time, McKeen's business boomed as UP and Southern Pacific fed him with large orders. Soon, serious problems developed with the Windsplitters that revealed fundamental flaws in McKeen's engineering, and his business dropped off. He sold most of his cars between 1909

---

dreary heavyweight cars with stodgy interior appointments hauled by steam locomotives had lost their appeal. The traveling public viewed these trains as slow and old-fashioned. Automobiles and airplanes were the new way to go, if you could afford to go at all. These new modes were faster, fashionable, and fun. UP wanted to make its trains more like the competition—swift, stylish, and sexy—and cheaper to operate.

UP had some pretty tall demands. It hoped to build a type of train that could outperform conventional steamers by a long margin—one that could run nonstop for 500 miles while

maintaining high speeds, allowing the railroad to trim transcontinental runs by a day or more. UP also desired greater fuel efficiency, and, since funds were tight, the UP board did not want to spend a lot on the new train either. A decade earlier these parameters would have been considered ludicrous, but recent technological advances made UP's dreams plausible.

The key lay in UP's experimentation with motorcars in the 1920s, notably its McKeen "windsplitter" railcars (sidebar). Although these self-propelled, gas-powered cars suffered from technical flaws that had greatly curtailed

A handful of U.S. railroads operated McKeen railcars, an early internal-combustion vehicle which embodied crude attempts at streamlining. Knifelike noses and portholed windows were their hallmarks. With bell ringing vigorously, a UP McKeen car trots along, probably near Denver in the 1920s. *Otto C. Perry, Denver Public Library, Western History Department*

and 1912, and the advent of World War I in 1914 decimated his business. Among the most serious flaws of the McKeen cars were poor engine placement and the mechanical transmission. The engine rode on the truck which subjected it to severe jarring. The transmission was inappropriate to the car's design and weight, and the cars were notorious for rough starts and burned out clutches. His very last car was constructed in 1917, and three years later Union Pacific absorbed McKeen's assets, allowing him to retire comfortably. Despite their flaws, some McKeen cars survived on local runs into the 1930s. McKeen himself lived until 1946, witnessing the railroad industry's streamliner revolution which he directly inspired.

Several McKeen employees went on to make significant contributions to the railroad industry based on their early work on his railcars. One of these was Edward G. Budd, founder of the Budd Company which built Burlington's streamlined *Zephyrs*, followed by a whole line of streamlined passenger cars. In the 1950s, Budd introduced the most successful of all American-built self-propelled railcars, the Rail Diesel Car or RDC—or sometimes just simply known as a Budd car.

their use, the basic concept behind them was valid. During the 1920s and 1930s there had been a variety of significant advances in internal-combustion technology. A. H. Fetters, a Union Pacific industrial engineer who had worked with the McKeen Car Company, had furthered petroleum fuel research in an effort to develop a better engine. In 1926, UP sent Fetters to Europe to learn about diesel developments. His results influenced UP's pioneering work on what would become America's first lightweight, streamlined train. As UP was contemplating its streamliner, new, more-powerful internal-combustion engines were

being developed. All the technological pieces were there but had not been put together yet.

The internal-combustion-powered, streamlined train fit UP's vision for revamped passenger services, and the railroad, working with Pullman Car & Manufacturing Company and fledgling gas-electric motorcar builder Electro-Motive, helped pioneer the concept.

In 1933, the Century of Progress exposition in Chicago was a crucial event where ideas coalesced to bring about the development of the first streamlined trains. UP was not the only railroad interested in a streamliner. Long-time competitor Chicago, Burlington & Quincy had also expressed a keen interest, and the two railroads began a race to debut America's first lightweight, streamlined train.

UP vice-president of engineering E. E. Adams oversaw the new train's design. Wind-tunnel tests were performed by the University of Michigan on UP's behalf, while Pullman designed an aerodynamic train body that had minimal wind resistance at high speeds. Instead of steel, Pullman chose to construct the train out of aluminum, a metal commonly used in aircraft manufacture but virtually unknown in railcar construction. The resulting train would be a sharp contrast to the typical steam-powered trains of the period.

To power the speedster, UP had hoped to harness one of Electro-Motive's new two-cycle Winton 201 stationary diesel engines that had been successfully demonstrated at the Century of Progress. However, as the train was nearing completion in early 1934, Winton's demonstration engines had yet to be suitably tested for mobile applications. UP was anxious to beat Burlington and elected to use a 12-cylinder 600-hp. Winton distillate spark-ignition engine

instead of waiting for the diesel. Distillate was an inexpensive petroleum fuel, cheaper to manufacture than gasoline, but slightly more expensive than diesel fuel.

On February 12, 1934, Pullman, Electro-Motive, and UP unveiled the first American high-speed, streamlined, internal-combustion passenger train: Union Pacific's M-10000 (UP at the time was using "M"-numeric designations for all its motor-powered railcars). The three-car train employed a lightweight tubular design similar to that used on aircraft. The underbody supported the superstructure, which was covered by a thin, riveted, aluminum skin. The train exhibited an unusually

low profile—it was just 11 feet tall, more than two feet shorter than conventional passenger equipment—and featured a remarkable low-slung profile that rode just 9.5 inches over the the rail. Eight axles carried the train's three cars in an format known as "articulation." In this arrangement, adjoining cars shared bogies (truck assemblies) and were semi-permanently coupled. Articulation minimized slack action, reduced train oscillation, and—perhaps most importantly—allowed for a great weight reduction by eliminating several sets of heavy steel wheels, couplers, and related equipment. The entire train—dubbed "Little Zip" by UP people—weighed just 85 tons, approximately equal to the weight of a single heavyweight Pullman car.

It was an amazing-looking machine. At the head of its sleek streamlined body was an ominous face with a mouthlike grille and eyelike turret cab windows, making the train appear like some sort of ravenous racing caterpillar.

The M-10000 fulfilled and exceeded its designers ambitious expectations. It could reach 111 mph on level track. It had a long reach, being able to run for some 900 miles between fueling stops; nor did it need to stop every couple of hours to take on water as did steam locomotives. The M-10000 was inexpensive to operate, and its fuel costs were about a third of a comparable-size steam-powered train. But best of all, it was fun to ride, and the public was fascinated by it.

Union Pacific made the most of its new toy as a public-relations tool. Shortly after its well-publicized debut, UP sent the M-10000 on a 12,625-mile publicity tour of the U.S. It traveled from city to city, pausing 68 times to awe the public. Nearly two million people walked through the streamliner. Billed as "Tomorrow's Train Today," the M-10000 was a bold

new vision of the future that offered hope to people suffering from the Great Depression. Numerous public officials and celebrities availed themselves of the opportunity to be seen with it, as the train itself had very quickly had become a national celebrity in its own right. Even U. S. President Franklin D. Roosevelt toured the train. In 1934, the M-10000 visited the ongoing Century of Progress exhibition in Chicago—appropriately so, as for all practical purposes the train was a fruit of the exhibition's inspiration.

UP soon announced that it had ordered additional trains for regular service (in fact, it had ordered the next train, the M-10001, while the M-10000 was still under construction). However, once the M-10000 had finished its famous national tour, UP assigned it to a relatively obscure run. Now operating as *The Streamliner* and later as the *City of Salina*, it ran between Kansas City, Missouri, and Salina, Kansas, on UP's old Kansas Pacific.

Why such an ignominious fate for such a successful, well-liked train? UP had initially contemplated using the train in a high-speed, 24-hour Chicago–Los Angeles service, complete with a sleeping car that had been built but not operated with the train during its barnstorm tour. In some ways the M-10000 was limited by the very features that made it a success. Its short, inflexible consist only had 116 seats, hardly enough to accommodate the hordes of people that—as indicated by its tour reception—hoped to ride it. It was ill-suited for a heavily traveled route and thus assigned to a less-populated run. Also, the railroad undoubtedly wanted to monitor the new train's daily performance and maintain a low profile in case of embarrassing mishaps. The M-10000's short career was quite successful, however, and in 1935 UP reported

America's first long-distance streamliner was the M-10001 train, which became the Chicago–Portland *City of Portland* in 1935. The train is posing near 42nd Street in Omaha during its pre-inaugural press trip in 1935. The train was delivered in 1934 and modified with a higher-horsepower engine before entering revenue service. *Union Pacific Museum Collection, image No. 62-115*

The new *City of Denver* with the backup M-10003 powercar set is shown leaving Denver in the late 1930s. This is a fine example of the later M-series streamliners that featured the automobile-style power cars. Futuristic trains like this gave hope to an America beset by the Great Depression. *Otto C. Perry, Denver Public Library, Western History Department*

INSET: In the late 1930s, UP advertised its streamliner fleet in a special folder that showed each train and its equipment. *Mike Schafer collection*

that *The Streamliner* was carrying 280 passengers daily. The train's Winton distillate engine had permitted the UP to debut the M-10000 ahead of Burlington's *Zephyr*—which became the first *diesel-powered* streamliner—but, the engine was unusual and less reliable than later designs. The cost of replacing it with a diesel power plant was deemed prohibitively high, so UP retired the train in 1941 and scrapped it for the war effort. Burlington's famous *Zephyr* 9900, which had debuted only two months after UP's train, enjoyed a much longer career. It worked in regular service for a quarter of a century and is now on display at the Chicago Museum of Science and Industry.

THE STREAMLINER FLEET GROWS

The M-10000's instant success laid a fertile ground for more trains to follow, and within a few months of the M-10000's unveiling, Union Pacific introduced the six-car M-10001. This train resembled the M-10000 but featured a 900-hp. Winton 201-A diesel engine, making it UP's first diesel-powered streamliner. Whereas the M-10000 was a coach train best-suited for short-distance service and demonstration runs, the M-10001 had three sleeping cars and a buffet-coach, making it the world's first long-distance,

diesel-electric powered streamliner. However, before the M-10001 entered revenue service, it worked as a publicity vehicle. On October 22, 1934, the M-10001 set out on its most famous journey, departing Los Angeles for an express run to New York City. It ran cross country in just 56 hours and 55 minutes, arriving at New York Central's Grand Central Terminal on October 25 amid great celebration. In 1934, this was an amazing feat. The train had beaten the previous land speed record, set in 1906, by roughly 14.4 hours and was nearly a full day faster than regularly scheduled passenger trains of the time.

UP proudly introduced the M-10001 as part of its regular passenger fleet, designating it on May 5, 1935, as the *City of Portland*. Its sleepers were appropriately named for E. H. Harriman, Abraham Lincoln, and the Oregon Trail, reflecting a historical connection between the new train and its Chicago–Portland run.

According to Arthur Dubin in his book *Some Classic Trains*, the M-10001 *City of Portland* set traveled the 2,272 miles between Chicago and its namesake city in just 39.5 hours, cutting 18 hours off the fastest earlier schedules. From start to stop, the train averaged 57 mph. To maintain a sustained pace over such a long distance, especially considering the amount of mountain-running involved, was phenomenal for the period. The M-10001 set was later upgraded with a 1,200-hp. engine and rebuilt as a seven-car train.

In June 1935, UP ordered additional articulated trains with longer consists to provide even greater passenger capacity. UP's third train, No. M-10002, entered service as the *City of Los Angeles* on May 15, 1936. Its power-car set contained two Winton engines generating a total 2,100 hp. A month later, Union Pacific debuted its M-10004 *City of San Francisco* streamliner. While the M-10001 and M-10002 resembled the M-10000, the power-car set on this newest train featured a distinctive, handsome nose treatment that resembled GM's automobile designs of the period. Union Pacific's last fully articulated streamliners were the M-10005 and M-10006, providing daily *City of Denver* service between Chicago and the Mile High City. These trains resembled the M-10004, but operated with 12 to 14 cars. At least one of the trains was set up to operate with three Winton engines and developed 3,600 hp. A seventh locomotive-only set, designated M-10003, was built as back-up power for the *City of San Francisco*. Although these trainsets were purchased for specific runs, they wound up in later years working in various services. For example, the M-10002 worked in later years as a backup for the *City of Denver*.

UP's six articulated trains along with Burlington's *Zephyr*s set an important precedent that introduced American railroading to diesel-powered passenger trains and lightweight, streamlined equipment. The streamliners attracted the public's attention to the railroad, carried full loads, and were indeed comparatively inexpensive to operate. However, operational inflexibility and other difficulties associated with articulated train design, combined with the development of standardized "off-the-shelf" diesel-electric locomotives and non-articulated lightweight streamlined passenger cars precluded UP (and most other roads) from further embracing the articulated format. The new order of business was to order fleets of locomotives and build a "pool" of passenger cars that could be drawn from for whatever service necessary. Fixed-consist trains reduced a railroad's ability to adjust a train's size to accommodate peaks and valleys in customer demand.

The *City of San Francisco* became one of Union Pacific's most famous streamlined trains, arguably second only to the *City of Los Angeles*. Ironically, the train never actually reached its namesake city, terminating instead at the Oakland waterfront. From there, passengers were obliged to take ferries and, later, dedicated buses to downtown San Francisco. When new, the *COSF* was by far the heaviest and longest streamliner on any railroad. It weighed 520 tons and stretched to 725 feet, making it more than three times as long as the M-10000. It carried four sleeping cars, each named to invoke images of Hawaii to symbolize the *City's* connection with luxurious Pacific steamships. The *City of San Francisco* was jointly run by Union Pacific, Southern Pacific, and Chicago & North Western, but since it was mostly a UP operation, it carried UP colors—although the SP and C&NW heralds appeared on the power cars.

Period advertisements boasted the train took just "39¾ hours Chicago to San Francisco." This bettered the best steam-hauled schedule by an amazing 19 hours—an especially impressive run for the period. In test runs, the M-10004 attained a top speed of 115 mph, although in regular service it was limited

To accommodate the extra travelers heading for the world's fair in San Francisco in 1939, UP dolled up two steam locomotives with streamlined shrouding and upgraded heavyweight cars to launch the new *Forty-Niner*. The Chicago–Oakland train served as a supplement to *City of San Francisco* service which, at the time, only had one trainset and thus could make only five round trips to California per month. The *Forty-Niner* is shown on exhibition at Green River, Wyoming, with its shrouded 4-8-2 locomotive. Local folks (left in photo) have come down to the depot to see the new train. *UP, Dave Oroszi collection*

to 95 mph—although there is little doubt that, when necessary, skilled engineers made up lost time with some extra fast running!

Initially, the *City of San Francisco* departed Chicago in early evening and arrived at San Francisco Bay before 8 A.M. of the second morning (missing all the great scenery of Donner Pass, unfortunately). Departure back east was usually the following day in a late-afternoon time slot with a second-morning arrival in Chicago. Since there was but a single set of equipment at the onset of *City of San Francisco*

service, daily departures were impossible. Rather, the train was advertised as having five "sailings" per month in each direction, with sailing dates established in advance and published in timetables.

The popularity of the first *City of San Francisco* and *City of Los Angeles* prompted Union Pacific to order two completely new trains to accommodate demand. But the fixed consists of those early trains also prompted UP to order equipment sets comprised of 17 commercially designed, interchangeable, non-articulated

A rare color view of a prewar-edition *City of Los Angeles* shows the famous streamliner in all its grandeur at Riview, Wyoming, in 1946. One of Electro-Motive's unusual E2 locomotives leads two E6 boosters on an exceptionally long train. Service men and women were still returning from wartime duties. *Union Pacific Museum Collection, image No. 76270*

streamlined passenger cars. Instead of a stylized power car designed specifically for each train, the new equipment sets were hauled by independent diesel-electric locomotives that, theoretically, could be assigned to any passenger train, heavyweight or streamlined—although when delivered they were lettered for *City of Los Angeles* and *City of San Franciso* service (the lettering was later removed). These changes greatly improved operating flexibility.

Built in 1937–38, the new trains had 40 percent more capacity than the older articulated sets and featured several noteworthy improvements, including themed club cars. The new *City of Los Angeles*' crown jewel was the *Little Nugget*, a dormitory-club car designed by Walt Kuhn to resemble an old West saloon—complete with fake gas lamps and a mechanical canary in a gilded cage (reportedly eventually pulverized by a well-aimed spray from a seltzer bottle). The new equipment augmented the first *COLA* trainset, allowing UP to double the number of sailings each month. Meanwhile, the new *City of San Francisco*

modern, restful pullmans and coaches

● Whether you travel by Pullman or Coach, the modern equipment adds to the pleasure of your journey. Pullman accommodations include berths, roomettes and bedrooms. In the modern Coaches, as shown on the right, all seats must be reserved in advance.

Bedrooms offer privacy, comfort and safety.

Coach seats have adjustable, reclining backs and stretch-out leg rests for day and night comfort.

Beverage and lounge service is available.

A 1964 brochure for the Domeliner *City of St. Louis* illustrated the train's colorful, homey accommodations. UP heavily promoted its trains almost to the end. *Mike Schafer collection*

Back-to-back Electro-Motive E6s hustle along with the heavyweight *Pony Express* at an unknown location, but probably near Denver, circa 1940. The *Pony* was a secondary run on a Kansas City–Denver–Los Angeles routing. *Otto C. Perry, Denver Public Library, Western History Department.*

equipment replaced the M-10004 set, which was promptly rebuilt and reassigned to *City of Los Angeles* service. In 1941 the demand for streamlined service warranted two more sets for these *City* trains, allowing the *COSF* to double its monthly sailings. After World War II, UP had accumulated enough new rolling stock to make the *City of Los Angeles, City of San Francisco*, and the *City of Portland* daily.

In July 1937, UP, C&NW, and SP launched the all-Pullman *Forty-Niner*, a weekly, semi-streamlined train between Chicago and Oakland. Union Pacific dressed up two steam locomotives, a Pacific (4-6-2) and a Mountain (4-8-2), in handsome, streamlined shrouding painted golden brown and Armour yellow. The cars carried names that reflected California's gold-rush days.

During the busy summer season of 1939 and 1940, yet another train, the *Treasure Island Special*, was added to the Overland Route to accommodate passengers visiting the Golden Gate Exposition at Treasure Island in San Francisco Bay. Both the *Forty-Niner* and *Treasure Island Special* were discontinued with the onset of World War II.

The overwhelming success of its streamliners encouraged UP to closely scrutinize its other passenger services. If simply introducing a handful of slick, speedy, new trains caused passenger traffic to jump by more than 30 percent, imagine what would happen if serious attention were paid to traditional long-distance services? Since it was obvious that one way or another, the day of the drab, old Pullman car was slowly coming to a close, UP was determined to make the best of the situation

and innovate. It wanted to appeal more to middle-class passengers and the growing Western tourist trade. UP did so by taking another radical new step in the passenger business, defying conventional patriarchal wisdom by hiring a woman consultant to do market research on what passengers wanted from train travel. Then UP designed a new service (but using older, upgraded equipment) based on the input. The result was the coach-and-Pullman *Challenger*, introduced in 1935 between Chicago and Los Angeles. Although the *Challenger* was a conventionally configured steam-powered train, it featured modernized interiors that were cheery and brightly lit and implemented a new attitude on the part of the railroad and its crew. The train was reasonably priced and offered basic amenities aimed at the middle-class family passenger. UP employed women nurses as stewardesses and assigned cars exclusively for women traveling alone or with children in an effort to better attract female passengers. The *Challenger* was an instant success and inspired similar trains to San Francisco and Portland.

After World War II, UP reorganized its transcontinental schedules, cancelled the *Challenger* along with other affordable sleeper trains, and refocused its energy on premier streamliners, which were being put on to daily schedules. Nonetheless, the railroad restored the *Challenger* name in 1954 by introducing a new all-streamlined consist in the place of the aged *Los Angeles Limited*—the traditional heavyweight train that had served for nearly half a century. Sadly, though, by this time the tide was turning against the long-distance passenger train.

After the war, UP purchased more lightweight equipment and diesels and greatly expanded its streamliner services. In 1946, UP added the *City of St. Louis*, which operated over the Wabash between St. Louis and Kansas City, then ran westward across the Kansas Pacific to Denver and on to Cheyenne where it passed connecting cars to Los Angeles-, Oakland-, and Portland-bound trains. In 1951 UP extended the train all the way to Los Angeles.

In May 1947, General Motors and Pullman-Standard unveiled the *Train of Tomorrow*, a pocket streamliner comprised of four brand-new dome cars hauled by a single Electro-Motive E7 passenger diesel. The train was designed to promote train travel while

An A-B-B set of Electro-Motive E8s lead the domed version of the *City of Los Angeles* past Castle Rock in Utah's Echo Canyon. The addition of dome cars to the *City of Los Angeles* in the mid 1950s arguably made this final edition of a great train the best of all editions. The train's dome diners were among the finest dining cars ever to roll on any American rails. *UP, Dave Oroszi collection*

Following a dispute with Overland partner Chicago & North Western, Overland Route passenger trains were shifted to the Milwaukee Road between Chicago and Omaha in October 1955. On a summer night in 1966, the combined westbound *City of Los Angeles/City of San Francisco/ Challenger* pauses at the Milwaukee Road depot in Savanna, Illinois. UP power normally worked through to Chicago. *Ron Lundstrom*

introducing America to the dome-car concept (although Burlington had already done this in 1945). For three years it traveled the country and thrilled passengers and observers in the same fashion that the M-10000 had done during the Great Depression. UP bought the *Train of Tomorrow* in 1950 and assigned it to the Portland–Seattle route.

The dome car made a distinct impression with train riders, and UP's transcontinental competitors—mainly the Burlington-Rio Grande-Western Pacific *California Zephyr,* Santa Fe's *Super Chief,* and Milwaukee Road's *Olympian Hiawatha*—were quick to embrace this novel new wonder. Curiously, UP lagged behind instituting transcontinental dome service, waiting until 1955 to introduce "Astra Domes" on the *City of Portland* and *City of Los Angeles.* UP bought 15 dome lounge-observation cars and 10 dome diners from American Car & Foundry, and then went all out in marketing them. Among the most well-known marketing coups included plugs for the UP and its new domes in two episodes of the hit sitcom of the 1950s, "I Love Lucy," including one very brief scene with William Frawley and Vivian Vance (Fred and Ethel Mertz) filmed in the lower level of a dome lounge-observation car. (The remaining scenes were filmed on stage sets.)

PARKS AND PASSENGERS

Union Pacific was ideally suited to bring passengers to some of America's most famous

national parks, including Bryce Canyon, Zion, the Grand Canyon, and Yellowstone. In addition, UP built and operated one of America's earliest and best-known ski resorts—Idaho's Sun Valley—which it developed to boost ridership and help advertise the railroad. (The UP and Sun Valley was also plugged in an episode of the "Lucy-Desi Comedy Hour" in the late 1950s.) The famous resort was some 70 miles north of Shoshone, Idaho, on the Ketchum branch. Sun Valley was originally intended as an exclusive resort for winter sports but was later expanded into an all-weather vacation resort aimed at both wealthy and middle-class vacationers. Its Challenger Inn offered comfortable, affordable lodging.

UP's Utah Parks subsidiary handled tours of the spectacular Bryce Canyon and Zion National parks as well as the Cedar Breaks National Monument where UP operated its Cedar Breaks Lodge. UP was integral to the development of these scenic, though often remote, areas to the public. Prior to the advent of good roads, the railroad was the safest and most practical way to visit these parks. UP operated special trains for vacationers over its Cedar City branch to Cedar City which served as the gateway to the Utah Parks. Motor coaches filled the gap between trainside and the various lodges and hotels within the parks.

Pocatello, Idaho, served as UP's gateway to Yellowstone, the Grand Tetons, and the Craters of the Moon National Monument. The seasonal *Yellowstone Special* operated as a connection between mainline trains at Pocatello and West Yellowstone.

DECLINE TO AMTRAK

Through deft marketing, continued service improvements, new rolling stock, and faster, more frequent trains, UP had succeeded in rescuing its passenger service from the depths of Depression-era lows. However, by the 1950s, passenger ridership began to decline again on a nationwide scale. In the years immediately following World War II, falling oil prices, cheap automobiles, an emerging airline industry, and general economic prosperity set the stage for another decline. Then, in the mid-1950s, the advent of the government-sponsored interstate and jet airliner just about wiped out passenger trains altogether.

The UP had recovered from the Depression-era loses, but by the mid-1950s it was becoming apparent that passenger-related investments weren't paying off as quickly and successfully (if at all) as they had 20 years earlier. Like most other railroads around the country, UP was again looking for ways to stem falling patronage and at the same time reduce operating costs. Perhaps it was time to reinvent the streamliner.

In 1956, not long after UP's 1930s-era streamliners had run off their last miles, General Motors unveiled its futuristic *Aerotrain*. GM felt it had cleverly melded highway and railway technology which it advertised would "revolutionize rail travel." The train employed a racy, streamlined, lightweight locomotive built by GM's Electro-Motive Division (EMD) that pulled a non-articulated set of modified bus bodies (from GM's Motor Coach Division) riding on railroad wheels.

UP tested one of the two *Aerotrains* that had been built, assigning it to L.A.–Las Vegas service as the *City of Las Vegas* to capitalize on the growing gambler trade. Despite good intentions, the *Aerotrain* was flawed. Passengers complained about its rough-riding characteristics and the smaller, more-confining carbodies. The train was also underpowered, requiring a helper to surmount Cajon Pass. The *Aerotrain* ran on the UP from December 18, 1956, until September 14, 1957, when it was replaced by conventional equipment.

Following this brief fling with new train concepts, UP faced the realities of the day: declining ridership was probably irreversible, and perhaps the best approach was to simply reduce costs. Train consolidation was one quick and relatively easy approach. After the high-travel season of 1956, the *Challenger* was combined with the *City of Los Angeles* during the off seasons, and in 1962 UP combined its famous *Overland* with the *City of San Francisco*. By the end of 1969, all of the remaining Chicago-based *City* streamliners ran combined east of North Platte.

To UP's credit, its trains remained classy right to the end, and although it trimmed service, most of its major routes featured at least one decent passenger train until Amtrak assumed most intercity passenger train operations on May 1, 1971. Only a Chicago–Oakland service then plied UP rails. In later years service was restored to Portland and Los Angeles via UP rails, and Amtrak has variously operated over other Union Pacific routes. However, by 1997, budget cuts and route restructuring had again eliminated most intercity passenger service from UP's traditional main lines. Today Union Pacific's famed Overland Route is void of passenger trains; it is traveled solely by the seemingly endless parade of freights.

The eastbound *City of Denver* has just arrived North Platte during the Christmas holiday season of 1970—the last Christmas season that UP would serve its traveling public. The train will be combined here with the *City of Los Angeles/City of San Francisco* before continuing to Chicago. Alas, passengers aboard the *City of Denver* on this evening had a long wait ahead of them, as the California trains were over three hours tardy. *Mike Schafer*

Developed by the UP, the 4-12-2 wheel arrangement appropriately became known as the Union Pacific type. These hulking locomotives featured three cylinders (the third cylinder is visible tucked back above the pilot) and at the time of their reign were the largest non-articulated steam locomotives in North America. The 9000 is shown during break-in tests in 1926. *Brian Solomon collection*

6
THE OVERLAND ROUTE

The Steam World of Union Pacific

BIG STEAM AND UP ARE SYNONYMOUS

On a clear May 10, 1869, Union Pacific's No.119 made history when it posed pilot-to-pilot with Central Pacific's *Jupiter* in that fabulous ceremony marking the completion of the transcontinental railway. Photographers working with unwieldy wet-plate cameras carefully documented this grand event, making dozens of photos from all angles featuring these two locomotives. There is little doubt that these images are the most often reproduced and well-remembered railway photographs ever taken. Today, Union Pacific 119 remains one of the most famous locomotives in the world.

EARLY STEAM

The irony of the above event is that neither UP's 119 nor CP's *Jupiter* were intended to pose at Promontory. Central Pacific's prized *Antelope* was damaged en route to the festivities, while Union Pacific's highly polished intended locomotive was unable to attend account of being stranded by a washout many miles east of the celebration. Instead, UP had to settle for lowly No. 119, a common 4-4-0 of the period, built for freight service. Undoubtedly this was a letdown for Union Pacific, which hoped to show off its finest engine at its most-celebrated event. However, it was a blessing for locomotive historians and the general public because when we see these famous photographs, we are looking at typical, everyday locomotives of the period instead of atypical dandies. These two specimens are exactly the sort of locomotives that would have operated over the line on a day-to-day basis.

Given this knowledge, it is remarkable that these locomotives were so highly decorated and colorful. But, locomotives of this period were sparkling, shiny, colorfully painted, ornately decorated machines. These were more than just utilitarian transport devices; they were the pride of the railway and the symbol of industrial advancement and man's conquest of the American West. They were adorned in the elaborate styling of the Victorian age. Locomotives were designed for simplicity of operation and maintenance, but with exceptionally detailed decoration. They were intended as things of beauty, so every element of the locomotive was decorated to make it as attractive as possible. Decorative ironwork was used to support the headlamp while ornamental brass was used to cover cylinders, check valves, and other machinery. Russian iron covered the boiler, cabs were made of the finest hardwood, decorated with gingerbread trimmings and covered in thick lacquer, while the wheels, pilots, and tenders were painted in brilliant colors. Often detailed decorative murals were painted on the sides of the tenders, headlamps, and sand domes.

Number 119 was one of five locomotives (Nos. 116–120) built by the Rogers Locomotive Works of Paterson, New Jersey, in 1868. In the 1860s, Rogers was one of the most respected American locomotive builders and famous for its high-quality locomotives and glamorous decorations. Union Pacific paid about $13,000 for each of these five locomotives, using them for construction of the railroad and later in freight service. Each locomotive weighed about 64,000 pounds, burned coal, and featured a straight "shotgun" smokestack. It is unknown what colors No. 119 actually wore at Promontory in May 1869, but it is commonly portrayed in crimson, wine red, and deep olive

89

paint with gold trimmings—common colors for the period, and reflective of the treatment of a similar UP locomotive whose colors are known.

In many respects Union Pacific's early steam was typical of the average American railroad in the second half of the nineteenth century. Although it owned few unusual locomotives, a cross section of its roster revealed a fairly standard array of locomotives. After the end of the Civil War, many railroads switched from wood to coal, and by 1890 most mainline American locomotives were coal-burners. UP's were no exception, and while some UP locomotives were wood-burners, many used coal from an early date. The dearth of timber along UP's east-west main line, combined with ample coal deposits along the route, played a significant role in the choice of fuel.

Union Pacific traversed windy, dry country, and its locomotives used a great variety of elaborate smokestacks to minimize spark emissions and smoke from blowing into the cab of the engine. In UP's first two decades, balloon and diamond stacks were common on its locomotives as well as the unusual Congdon stack. Toward the end of the century, straight shotgun stacks and other less elaborate varieties were typical.

UP purchased locomotives from a number of builders, including Baldwin, Brooks, Cooke, Manchester, Norris, Rogers, and Schenectady. During the mid-1880s, the railroad's Omaha Shops began rebuilding older locomotives, and in the 1890s it began

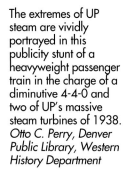

The extremes of UP steam are vividly portrayed in this publicity stunt of a heavyweight passenger train in the charge of a diminutive 4-4-0 and two of UP's massive steam turbines of 1938. *Otto C. Perry, Denver Public Library, Western History Department*

producing new locomotives. One anomaly on the Union Pacific in its early years were a handful of Camelbacks with Wootten fireboxes, a locomotive more commonly found on Eastern lines whose locomotives burned clean-burning Anthracite coal which required extra-large fireboxes.

AMERICANS

Like most railroads of the time, UP had a large number of 4-4-0 Americans, such as its famous No. 119. The American type—often called the American Standard—was the most popular locomotive of the nineteenth century. It was introduced in the mid 1830s and was widely built after 1850 because its specifications were especially well-suited to early American railroads. It was a powerful, compact locomotive with four driving wheels and riding on a three-point suspension system using a pivoting four-wheel pony (leading) truck. This gave the engine remarkable flexibility, which was necessary for successful operation on often lightly built American tracks. The American type is best remembered in its classical form with a prominent "cow catcher" pilot, conical "balloon" smokestack, and bright coloring.

The specific details of many Union Pacific early locomotives have been lost over time, but there is an extraordinary amount of information available on UP's 4-4-0 *Seminole*, thanks to Alfred Bruce who reprinted the locomotive's specifications in his book *The Steam Locomotive in America*. It was built in 1867 by Rogers,

just a year before the 119, and is considered by Bruce and others to be a typical American locomotive built during the Civil War period.

By analyzing the *Seminole*'s dimensions, we can get a better understanding of both Union Pacific's locomotives in its formative period and of the size and power of typical American locomotives built during this time. This is especially valuable when compared with UP's truly gargantuan steam locomotives built 75 years later at the end of the steam era—some of the largest and most powerful steam locomotives ever built—demonstrating the tremendous growth in size and power of American locomotives. The *Seminole* used 16 x 22-inch cylinders (bore and stroke), rode on 54-inch driving wheels, weighed 62,000 pounds, and placed 42,000 pounds on its drivers. The locomotive had a 23-foot wheel base and was 14 feet 10 inches tall; its firebox had a 14.5-square-foot grate, and the boiler worked at 130 pounds per square inch. It delivered an estimated 10,700 pounds of tractive effort. UP's largest steam power, its famous Big Boys, were twelve and one half times heavier and delivered almost 13 times greater tractive effort than *Seminole*.

In the early years, 4-4-0s were used in all kinds of service, hauling mainline freight and passenger trains, but by the 1880s, as freight trains grew in size and weight, the 4-4-0 lost favor in mainline freight service to larger types. Yet, the American type survived on the UP in mainline passenger service for another decade and remained a valued locomotive for branch-line work and specialized service well into the twentieth century. The last UP 4-4-0 was not cut up until the early 1940s.

TEN-WHEELERS

In numbers, the 4-6-0 Ten-Wheeler-type was second only to the 4-4-0 American type on the Union Pacific—which was consistent with the national trend in locomotive ownership in the U.S. With its extra set of drivers, the 4-6-0 was a significantly more powerful locomotive than the 4-4-0. UP initially purchased 4-6-0s in 1867 for freight work in graded territory in Wyoming where greater power was needed to move trains. With their 57-inch drivers, the railroad's early 4-6-0s were well-suited for such high-tractive-effort applications. By the 1880s, UP had more than 100 4-6-0s and had become the railroad's standard freight locomotive. They held down mainline freight assignments for more than two decades but were gradually superseded on the main line by ever-larger and more-powerful locomotives. Union Pacific maintained the type for lighter work until nearly the end of steam. The 4-6-0 type survived on the UP for roughly 90 years, giving it the longest career of any steam locomotive type on the railroad.

CONSOLIDATIONS

The 2-8-0 Consolidation was another popular type on the UP. The railroad's first 2-8-0 was purchased from Baldwin in 1868 just a couple of years after the first "Consoli" was built for the Lehigh Valley, making UP among the earliest lines to use what was to be a very popular type of engine. At 90,000 pounds, this first engine was a monster compared to UP's other locomotives. It was built for grade-pulling service out of Cheyenne, and UP later purchased additional 2-8-0s for similar duties elsewhere in Wyoming and in Utah. By World War I, UP had acquired approximately 400 of the type, making them among the most common freight locomotives on the railroad. The early 2-8-0s featured the same sort of elaborate ornamentation and decoration as smaller locomotives, and used diamond stacks typical of the period.

Ten-Wheeler 1852 illustrates turn-of-the-century compound steam on the UP. Baldwin built this 79-inch-drivered 4-6-0 in 1900. It was rebuilt to a simple engine about 1916. *Baldwin*

Celebrating 50 years of service on the UP, 4-6-0 No. 25 smokes across the Los Angeles River with an excursion train of vintage wood coaches. Unfortunately, the date of this event was not noted on the photo, but it portrayed what UP steam looked like in action in the nineteenth century.

RARE EARLY TYPES

In its early years, Union Pacific used small numbers of less-common locomotive types, including 0-4-0 Ponies and 4-2-4 tank engines known as "Bicycles." UP also owned a variety of three-foot-gauge engines on various narrow-gauge lines that it acquired or was affiliated with, including the legendary Denver, South Park & Pacific. Toward the end of the nineteenth century, UP bought 15 4-8-0 Mastodon types from both Cooke and Brooks. In 1899 these 4-8-0s were Union Pacific's largest and most powerful locomotives. The Brooks locomotives employed boxy Belpaire boilers, unusual on American locomotives. The Belpaire boiler featured a prominent flat firebox crown sheet supported by both vertical and horizontal staybolts—a significantly different design than used by the far more common rounded "wagon top" boiler which is supported by radial staybolts. The Pennsylvania Railroad and Great Northern were large proponents of Belpaire boilers, but they were not common on Union Pacific or most other American lines.

The 4-8-0 never achieved widespread acceptance in the U.S. either, and the largest user of them was Southern Pacific. This wheel arrangement was just an anomaly in UP's otherwise fairly conventional roster, and most of them were disposed of in the 1920s. Initially 4-8-0s worked the territory where Union Pacific had always assigned its largest power—on Sherman and Archer hills, located on either side of Cheyenne. Later, some locomotives worked UP's grades in Idaho and Oregon.

NON-ARTICULATED COMPOUNDS

In a traditional steam engine, steam expands in the cylinder and is then exhausted into the atmosphere. This is inefficient and wastes remaining expansive power left in the steam. To take advantage of this wasted energy, the compound engine was designed to reuse the exhausted steam. A compound engine improves upon the thermal efficiency by double expansion of the steam through a system of high- and low-pressure cylinders, whereby exhausted steam from the high-pressure cylinders expands in low-pressure cylinders before finally exiting the engine.

The compound or double-expansion engine is a much more efficient device than a simple steam engine; it uses less steam to perform the same work as a simple engine and therefore burns less fuel and uses less water. A properly functioning compound locomotive may consume up to 20 percent less fuel and 50 percent less water than an equivalent simple locomotive.

This design was especially appealing to the Union Pacific because, when operating properly, the locomotives used less water and consumed less fuel, reducing locomotive operating costs. More-efficient locomotive operation was always an attractive prospect because locomotive costs represented a very large portion of a railway's total operating expenditure. The UP was one of many American railroads that acquired large numbers of non-articulated compound locomotives in the last decade of the nineteenth century and the early years of the twentieth century, operating them with varying success in both freight and passenger service.

Ultimately Union Pacific abandoned its non-articulated compounds, as did all American lines, when the cost of maintaining the compounds exceeded any savings obtained through improved efficiency. Since a compound is a more complicated machine, it has more moving parts and steam connections and thus requires more lubrication and maintenance than a conventional simple steam engine. Unless a compound is functioning properly, it will not operate with greater efficiency, so a higher level of maintenance is necessary than with simple engines.

Union Pacific's first compound locomotives were 2-8-0s from Schenectady Locomotive Works in 1890. These employed a two-cylinder cross-compound design, with a high-pressure cylinder on one side of the locomotive and low-pressure cylinder on the other. Around the turn of the century, UP purchased a number of Baldwin four-cylinder Vauclain compounds—initially, 2-8-0s for freight, and later high-drivered 4-4-2's for fast passenger service. The engine, developed by Samuel Vauclain, featured an arrangement of two sets of high-pressure and low-pressure cylinders, one atop the other with one set on each side of the locomotive. This arrangement was one of the more popular compound types in the U.S.

Harriman Standardization

After Edward H. Harriman took control of Union Pacific and then Southern Pacific and their various subsidiaries, he implemented a plan to purchase large numbers of locomotives using standard specifications for his various railroads. Standard designs reduced the cost of replacement parts and cut maintenance costs. Beginning in 1907, the Union Pacific Equipment Association was responsible for ordering most new power for Harriman's roads, and hundreds of locomotives were built for UP and SP under this arrangement. After Harriman

Sharing the turntable with a locomotive that would soon doom steam, 0-6-0 switcher No. 4466 is at Cheyenne in 1957. *John Dziobko*

died in 1909, standardization continued for a few more years but ended after the forced breakup of UP and SP by the Federal government. The Harriman standard locomotives were generally held in high regard, and many operated to the end of the steam era in the late 1950s.

ATLANTICS AND PACIFICS

The 4-4-2 Atlantic type was developed in the mid-1890s as a high-speed passenger locomotive and was typically built with very tall drivers. Union Pacific did not purchase any new Atlantics until after Harriman assumed control of the railroad in 1901. Under Harriman, the railroad modernized its locomotive fleet, acquiring many new locomotives. Unlike some lines that used Atlantics for passenger service before abandoning them for 4-6-2 Pacific types as trains grew larger and heavier, UP adopted a slightly different approach toward passenger locomotive procurement

and allocation. It bought both Atlantics and Pacifics simultaneously and tended to assign its 81-inch-drivered Atlantics to level territory—where they were well-suited for fast running—while it used Pacifics and 2-8-2 Mikados in mountain service where greater tractive effort was required.

The first Atlantics were ordered in 1903 and delivered the following year. The last of the type were Baldwin Vauclain compounds purchased in 1911 for service on Oregon-Washington Railway & Navigation lines, where greater power was required. The Atlantics performed well in their early years, but were ill-suited to handle heavier consists that had resulted from a growth in train length and the switch from wood to all-steel passenger equipment. Consequently, they were bumped by Pacifics from heavy runs and were retired during the 1920s and 1930s when larger locomotives were delivered.

The Pacific type had a significantly longer career than the Atlantic, although the nature of

The first of UP's 800-series Northerns line up at Council Bluffs, probably not long after the 4-8-4s were delivered in 1937. Enginemen in classic engineer garb appear to be comparing notes as their steeds await assignments. They were built primarily for passenger service. *UP, Dave Oroszi collection*

its assignments changed over the years. Initially, Pacifics were primarily assigned to passenger runs west of Cheyenne while the Atlantics were assigned to level runs. When more-powerful passenger locomotives arrived in the form of 4-8-2 Mountains in the early 1920s, Pacifics were bumped off premier runs in graded territory and re-assigned east of Cheyenne. Unlike the Atlantics that disappeared relatively early, the Pacifics survived until the mid-1950s, and a number were upgraded over the years, receiving energy saving improvements such as roller bearings, lightweight rods, and disc drivers.

In 1937 Union Pacific rebuilt two locomotives—a Pacific and a Mountain—with streamlined shrouds and painted them brown and Amour yellow for service on the Chicago–Oakland *Forty-Niner*. After that train was discontinued in 1941, the streamlined steam locomotives were assigned to other runs including the *San Francisco Overland Limited*

and the *Pacific Limited*. These were Union Pacific's only two streamlined steam locomotives. After a few years they were stripped of their shrouding.

MIKADOS

Union Pacific operated a large fleet of about 400 2-8-2 Mikados, making it one of the most common wheel arrangements on the railroad. It had 11 different classes of 2-8-2s. Early Mikados employed 57-inch drivers while later machines used 63-inch drivers. Although most American railroads used the "Mike" primarily as a heavy freight locomotive, UP bought a few specifically for mountain passenger service. During World War I, UP acquired 20 Mikados built to United States Railroad Administration (USRA) specifications. Despite their vast numbers and long service, only a few 2-8-2s survived to the end of steam operations. By 1958, there were just three left serviceable.

MOUNTAINS

The 4-8-2 Mountain type was first developed by the Chesapeake & Ohio to haul heavy passenger trains in graded territory. While other lines later adapted the type for other purposes, including fast freight service, Union Pacific adopted the 4-8-2 for essentially the same application as the C&O. Between 1922 and 1924 UP took delivery of 40 Mountains, 15 of which were assigned to the Los Angeles & Salt Lake. These locomotives replaced both Pacifics and the passenger-service Mikados on UP's steeply graded lines.

MALLETS

Baltimore & Ohio's famous "Old Maud," which used an 0-6-6-0 wheel arrangement, introduced the articulated Mallet compound type to American railroading in 1904. This large locomotive featured two complete sets of running gear under one large boiler. The type quickly caught on and initially were used as rear-end helper locomotives in heavy freight service. In 1906, Baldwin's Samuel Vauclain sold the Great Northern an order of Mallets with leading trucks designed to head freights over the Washington Cascades. The success of GN's locomotives resulted in the Mallets becoming a popular type for heavy, slow-speed freight service. Thousands were built for heavy service all around the U.S. using a variety of wheel arrangements.

In 1909 Union Pacific ordered six enormous 2-8-8-2 Mallet compounds for heavy freight

UP 4-8-4 No. 844 (for a time numbered 8444 so as not to conflict with a newer diesel of the same number) was never officially retired. For years following the steam era, the big Northern has served in various capacities including as an excursion engine and an ambassador for the UP. In this 1989 scene east of Grand Island, Nebraska, it is shown— attired in Overland gray—pulling revenue freight. *Brian Solomon*

service on its graded lines; three were assigned to the UP and three to its Oregon-Washington Railway & Navigation subsidiary. These early Baldwin Mallets met with limited success on the UP and no more were ordered. UP experimented with the Mallet compound again nearly a decade later when it ordered 15 2-8-8-0s from Alco in 1918. This Mallet type enjoyed much greater success than the earlier 2-8-8-2s, and UP placed several repeat orders. By the mid 1920s, the UP system had 70 2-8-8-0s in service. They primarily worked in mainline freight service across Wyoming where the steeply graded line had traditionally required the railroad's heaviest power.

Union Pacific's Mallet experience was atypical in that the 2-8-8-2 type was far more popular on a national scale than the 2-8-8-0. The 2-8-8-2 wheel arrangement represented 22.5 percent of all articulated steam locomotives built in the U.S. (710 locomotives, of which 624 were Mallet compounds), while the 2-8-8-0 represented just 6.6 percent of American articulated locomotives. So, although the UP bought roughly one-third of

the total production of 2-8-8-0s, it had less than 1 percent of the new 2-8-8-2s.

By the mid-1920s the slow-speed Mallet compound had fallen out of favor. UP, like many lines, was hoping to run faster freights and as a result invested in a fleet of three-cylinder locomotives while other railroads had taken an interest in the simple articulated type. The three-cylinder engine was very similar to the Mallet except that it fed high-pressure steam directly to both sets of running gear instead of the double expansion arrangement used in a Mallet compound. Union Pacific initially ignored this trend too, and did not order any new simple articulated locomotives until 1936 (when it developed the 4-6-6-4 for high-speed service), choosing to maintain its Mallets for mainline freight service for another decade. However, by 1937 the Mallets had begun to show their age and UP began converting them to simple operation.

At the end of World War II in 1945, Union Pacific was in desperate need for heavy power to accommodate the torrent of freight traffic traveling west over its main lines, so it purchased secondhand articulated locomotives from both Chesapeake & Ohio and Norfolk & Western. The C&O locomotives were simple articulateds built in mid 1920s while N&W's were USRA-designed 2-8-8-2 Mallet compounds from World War I. Both groups were lettered for UP and pressed into service on Sherman Hill west of Cheyenne. They filled UP's immediate need for power, but they did not last long after the crunch passed. After the war traffic levels eased and when new diesels began to arrive, these secondhand articulateds were among the first locomotives scrapped.

SANTA FE TYPES

The 2-10-2 wheel arrangement was commonly known as the Santa Fe type, but on the Union Pacific where the "Santa Fe" was the name of one of its fiercest competitors, these locomotives were just called 2-10-2s (two-ten-twos) and appropriately classed TTT. The 2-10-2 was expanded from a 2-10-0 Decapod by the Santa Fe in the early part of the twentieth century, and during World War I the 2-10-2 became a popular type for heavy freight service. UP first ordered the type from Baldwin in 1917 and initially assigned them between

Cheyenne and Ogden. Union Pacific was very pleased with the 2-10-2s' performance and ultimately ordered 185 of the type for use all over the system. They worked the Nevada desert grades on the Los Angeles & Salt Lake, shoved on the rear of heavy freights ascending California's Cajon Pass, lifted long drags over Encina, Telocasset, and Kamela summits in eastern Oregon, and hauled mile-long freights across Nebraska. All of UP's 2-10-2s were equipped with 63-inch drivers, and in later years some were fitted with disc drivers which allowed for better counter-balancing and permitted faster operation. These locomotives were built by all three major builders (Alco, Baldwin, and Lima) to UP specifications.

Forty 2-10-2s, Class TTT-6, Nos. 5040–5089, are noteworthy because they used Young valve gear and are believed to be the largest class of locomotives in North America so-equipped. Unlike the more common Walschaerts valve gear, which takes its motion from a combination of crosshead connection and an eccentric crank from one of the drivers, Young valve gear derives its motion solely from crosshead connections, making it one of the most unusual variety of outside valve gear in U.S. railroad applications.

Back in black-tie dress, the 844 assists UP's restored E-units on the "Royal Gorge Special," a special chartered run for members of the National Railway Historical Society en route from Denver to the NRHS national convention in Salt Lake City via UP's former-Rio Grande main line over Tennessee Pass. The special is shown in Utah's Price River Canyon on June 23, 1997. *Alex Mayes*

THREE-CYLINDER LOCOMOTIVES

The 844 and its kin were built for high-speed passenger service, and the famous Northern appears to be performing that service admirably on June 28, 1997, as it wheels a long, domed consist northward from Salt Lake City to Cache Junction, Utah. The occasion is an excursion for the NRHS convention at Salt Lake City. *Alex Mayes*

Traditionally, freight trains had plodded along at a steady slow pace, and even after almost 80 years of railway development and continuously improved locomotive designs, there had been no appreciable increase in freight train speed. Freight locomotive development had been aimed at building locomotives with greater tractive effort that were capable of hauling longer, heavier trains rather than faster ones. However, after World War I, railroads were feeling increased highway competition as improved roads and better trucks allowed for faster highway transportation. To better compete, American railroads responded by demanding faster freight locomotives. Several different solutions were offered by the locomotive builders. Alco's formula was the three-cylinder simple locomotive which it promoted between 1922 and 1930.

The advantages of a three-cylinder locomotive stemmed from reduced stress on pistons, crossheads, and main rods, afforded by dividing the power over three cylinders instead of just two. Reducing the stress allowed for lighter reciprocating parts. Also, the six power points on a three-cylinder locomotive, rather than just four on a conventional two-cylinder locomotive (reciprocating steam engines use double-acting pistons) gave the locomotive more even torque and smoother operation. This resulted in greater adhesion and higher

tractive effort than offered by a comparable two-cylinder engine, so a three-cylinder locomotive was less likely to slip when starting a train or when working a heavy grade. Alco employed this power advantage to achieve higher output and produce a faster, more powerful locomotive. The third cylinder, situated below the smokebox and between the two outside cylinders, powered a cranked axle. While the outside cylinders used a conventional Walschaerts valve-gear arrangement, the inside cylinder used a Gresley conjugated valve gear that took its motion from the outside piston valves and transmitted it using an arrangement of outside levers on the front of the locomotive. Alco built roughly 250 three-cylinder locomotives of which UP bought 98—the largest number of any railroad.

In 1925 UP bought a single 4-10-2 three-cylinder locomotive from Alco. This type was first used by Southern Pacific and was known as the Southern Pacific type on that road but as an Overland type on the UP. Union Pacific followed up with nine additional locomotives for service on the Los Angeles & Salt Lake. SP ordered a total of 49 4-10-2s , but UP only bought these ten and instead expanded the 4-10-2 design into a 4-12-2, known as the Union Pacific type. These impressive locomotives were classic UP: they were just simply

bigger than anything else. At the time, the railroad's 4-12-2s were the largest non-articulated locomotives in the U.S. and featured a 52-foot 4-inch wheel base—the longest ever used by a non-articulated North American locomotive.

UP's 4-12-2 weighed 495,000 pounds, placing 354,000 pounds on drivers. The outside cylinders were 24 x 32 inches while the inside cylinder was 25 x 31 inches. The 4-12-2 used 67-inch drivers, and the boiler operated at 220 PSI. The locomotive delivered 96,650 pounds of tractive effort and could produce an estimated 5,000 hp. They were initially intended for 35-mph operation—considered relatively fast for such a large machine—but proved they could maintain a steady 55 mph. No other American railroad ever ordered a 4-12-2

UP placed five orders for 4-12-2s between 1926 and 1930, a total of 88 locomotives. Originally, most were assigned to work west of Cheyenne. They were displaced from this run in 1936 by UP's 4-6-6-4 Challengers and then typically worked freight east of North Plate.

The 4-12-2s were more successful than that 4-10-2s, which were converted to two-cylinder operation in the 1940s before being scrapped. The 4-12-2s operated until the mid 1950s and were among the last steam retired. One locomotive was preserved and is displayed in Pomona, California.

Union Pacific's 4-6-6-4 Challengers were among the best-known steam locomotives in America. Challenger 3708 gets a spin on the turntable at Ogden in September 1957. It might be a sunny day in Utah, but it's twilight for nearly all UP steam. *John Dziobko*

One of UP's modern-day steam specialists leans out of Challenger 3985's cab during servicing in Houston, Texas, on June 11, 1995. *Tom Kline*

UP restored Challenger 3985 early in the 1980s and showed younger generations of Americans what articulated steam was all about. The 4-6-6-4 is shown making lots of smoke before dipping under the Texas Highway 79 overpass in the Brazos River valley while heading north along UP's Austin Subdivision on September 22, 1992. *Tom Kline*

UNION PACIFIC 800S

The 4-8-4 Northern type was first developed by the Northern Pacific in 1927 and was essentially an expansion of the 4-8-2 Mountain type. By the early 1930s, a number of North American railroads had adopted the 4-8-4 as both a passenger and freight locomotive. Its large firebox and high boiler capacity combined with tall drivers and a four-wheel leading truck made for a well-balanced locomotive that proved to be a very popular, modern design.

UP was slow to adopt the 4-8-4; rather, it was content to employ 4-8-2s and other types on its prime passenger runs. What is especially interesting from a technological perspective is that the UP finally adopted the 4-8-4 for passenger service several years *after* the successful debut of its famous diesel-powered streamlined trains. By the time UP's first 4-8-4s were being drawn up, it had one of the largest fleet of diesel-powered passenger trains in the world. So despite this apparent technological incongruity, UP perfected its 4-8-4 design, and today its Northerns are widely considered among the best ever built.

The railroad's first 4-8-4s, Nos. 800–819, were built by Alco in 1937. These modern locomotives used one-piece cast integral bed frames, lightweight reciprocating gear, roller bearings on all axles (a first for Union Pacific),

needle bearings on valves, and 77-inch box-pok drivers. They featured 24.5 x 32-inch cylinders. The railroad placed two additional orders of 4-8-4s with Alco, delivered in 1939 and 1944 respectively, and UP's later 4-8-4s were even more impressive than the first. They featured 80-inch drivers and 25 x 32 cylinders and operated at 300 psi boiler pressure.

UP's 800s were fast, powerful engines, designed to operate at a sustained 90 mph hauling a 1,000-ton passenger train. The drivers were precision counter balanced for 110 mph and could easily hit the 100 mph mark. William Kratville reports in his book, *Motive Power of the Union Pacific*, that unofficial records indicate that UP 841 raced across the

Nebraska Division at speeds of 105 to 112 mph hauling 25 heavyweight passenger cars. He cites another unofficial report, claiming an 800 reached the phenomenal speed of 130 mph! These speed reports are unconfirmed, and the methods of judging the locomotives speed are unknown, but they are impressive part of its legend. Officially the fastest steam locomotive in the world was achieved by London & North Eastern Railway's Class A4 Pacific *Mallard* which reached 126 mph in 1938.

The more relevant operating statistics were the 800s' especially high availability and service records. In their heyday the 800s regularly rolled approximately 15,000 miles a month, a figure that compares well with the best diesels of the period and significantly better than UP's 4-8-2s. On passenger trains, the 800s performed especially well in mountain service where they routinely outpaced their early diesel competition.

Although they were born in the diesel era, the 800s were typically assigned to premier passenger work all over the system but occasionally worked freight trains as well. Kratville indicates they could haul as many as 145 freight cars on the level Nebraska Division east of Omaha. By 1947 they began losing out to diesel power, yet survived in regular service until the mid 1950s. The UP never retired No. 844—the last UP 4-8-4 built—and it has run nearly every year since Alco built it in 1944.

Today it is one of the few steam locomotives still owned and operated by its original owner, and the UP is thus the only Class 1 railroad that has continuously had a steam locomotive on its roster since the inception of the railroad.

CHALLENGERS

The articulated steam locomotive had traditionally served as relatively slow-speed machine. The early Mallet compounds were particularly ponderous machines, respected for their exceptional pulling power, but not their speed. On most lines, Mallets would plod along at 10 to 15 mph hauling heavy freight over mountain grades or long weighty coal drags out of rural hollows in West Virginia or Utah. Santa Fe had experimented with high-speed Mallets in passenger service before World War I but soon abandoned the concept. In the 1920s the advent of the simple articulated locomotives resulted in somewhat speedier articulated engines, but even these would rarely operate faster than 40 mph.

In 1936 UP introduced the 4-6-6-4 type, representing a significant technological advance which elevated the articulated type from a slow-speed drag-hauling locomotive to a high-speed, general-purpose machine. Union Pacific's 4-6-6-4 overcame the two major impediments to fast operation: poor front-end stability and small drivers. By combining a four-wheel leading truck for better front-end stability, tall drivers that were easier to counter balance, and a high-capacity fire-box and boiler, Union Pacific had conceived a powerful, adaptable locomotive, capable of maintaining 70 mph with a heavy train.

The Challenger was born out of a need for a more flexible 12-coupled locomotive. UP's unique three-cylinder 4-12-2s had proven their merit running on the railroad's relatively curveless main lines in Nebraska and eastern Wyoming, but were ineffective on steep, twisting mountain lines farther west. By contrast, the 4-6-6-4, which featured 69-inch drivers and delivered 97,400 pounds of tractive effort, could operate on most Union Pacific main lines and it was well-suited for both freight and passenger work.

The Challengers were capable of hauling more than 7,000 tons on level ground. However, they were best-suited for graded running, and because of difficulties with turning the locomotives at the east end of the system, they

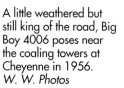

A little weathered but still king of the road, Big Boy 4006 poses near the coaling towers at Cheyenne in 1956. *W. W. Photos*

were rarely used on UP's level track across Nebraska. Typically they worked west of North Platte, especially on UP's grade-intensive Los Angeles & Salt Lake route. It was not unusual to see 4-6-6-4s hauling both freight and passenger trains on UP's Oregon lines, and they were often used on Portland passenger runs.

Unlike the 4-12-2 and the 4-8-8-4, which were unique to Union Pacific, the Challenger's flexibility made it a very popular, simple articulated type. Alfred Bruce, author of *The Steam Locomotive in America*, notes that 215 Challengers were built—105 of these for UP—making it one of the most numerous simple articulated locomotives in the U.S. In the West, they were used by Rio Grande, Northern Pacific, and Western Pacific, but they also enjoyed success on Eastern coal carriers Delaware & Hudson, Western Maryland, and Clinchfield.

The Challenger was largely the inspiration of UP's Assistant General Superintendent of Motive Power and Machinery, Otto Jabelmann.

Like almost all new locomotives, the Challenger was designed to reduce operating costs, so Jabelmann incorporated many elements of modern design elements intended to improve efficiency. UP's Challengers featured lightweight, alloy-steel reciprocating parts including side rods and main rods. Roller bearings were used on the locomotive and tender axles, and the boilers were originally made from manganese steel. The first Challengers were built as coal-fired locomotives and were equipped with automatic stokers. Although they were later converted to oil operation in the 1930s and 1940s, some were reconverted to coal in the mid 1950s.

Union Pacific made other changes to its Challenger fleet. Initially the Challengers had difficulties with the front engine slipping, so later locomotives were built with a slightly heavier front engine section. Some of the early locomotives were rebuilt with cast steel front-engine frames, replacing older built-up

Spanking new and shiny, Big Boy 4002 stands pristine at Omaha in 1941 while engine crews again compare their pocket watches. These were the locomotives that kids' dreams were made of when railroading was a major force in the American way of life and UP color publicity photos of Big Boys adorned classrooms from coast to coast. *UP, Dave Oroszi collection* frames. Difficulties with the manganese boilers resulted in UP installing new boilers made from carbon steel. A few locomotives were equipped with "elephant ear" smoke deflectors to minimize problems with smoke and noxious exhaust gases from entering the cab. In 1940 the Challenger design was improved with the introduction of the large, flat bearing surface for the forward engine to pivot on which minimized vertical motion, providing a much smoother ride at high speeds.

All of UP's Challengers were built by Alco, the railroad's preferred steam builder in later years. The first Challengers came with tenders that rode on pairs of six-wheel Buckeye trucks, but later orders used tenders with 14-wheel "Centipede" trucks.

Two Union Pacific Challengers escaped scrapping, and in the early 1980s UP restored No. 3985 to active service. It has toured the Union Pacific system in excursion service.

BIG BOYS

The success of the 4-6-6-4 Challenger led the UP to expand the concept into a 4-8-8-4 design. These enormous, magnificent machines are the world famous "Big Boys." Although these imposing locomotives certainly are some of the best-known steam locomotives ever made—and without doubt the most enduring legacy of Union Pacific's steam days—they are often frequently miscredited as the largest steam locomotive ever built. They briefly claimed this superlative when they were new, but they were soon surpassed by a slightly larger machine: Chesapeake & Ohio's monstrous 2-6-6-6 Allegheny built in 1942. The heaviest Big Boys weighed 772,000 pounds, but C&O's Alleghenies weighed 775,330 pounds. The reason for this confusion stems from C&O and the Allegheny's builder, Lima Locomotive Works, misrepresenting the weight of the 2-6-6-6 and reporting it as slightly less than the Big Boy's.

But, while the Big Boy might not hold the title as the heaviest steam locomotive, it is the longest. The engine has a wheelbase of 72 feet 5 inches and its length measures 85 feet 3 inches; but the length of the locomotive and tender is an astounding 132 feet 9 inches! The Big Boy's tremendous length, not weight, was its principal limiting factor in general operations. UP installed longer turntables at Ogden, Green River, Laramie, and Cheyenne to accommodate the Big Boys. The locomotives occasionally operated beyond these limits, but

not often because turning them elsewhere was so difficult.

The Big Boys were indeed big; in addition to their great length, they were 16 feet 2 inches tall. However, unlike most early enormous locomotives, they were not built as slow-speed machines. Like the Challengers, they were designed to operate at speeds up to 70 mph, and are reported to have run as fast as 80 mph. They routinely ran up to 60 mph but gave their best performance hauling freight in the 30–40 mph range. They could develop more than 7,000 hp. at these speeds—more power than even the most modern, alternating-current traction diesel-electrics operating today. They used 68-inch drivers, by far the largest on any locomotive ever built with 16 driving wheels,

and had four 23.75 x 32-inch cylinders. The boiler operated at 300 psi and the locomotive produced 135,375 pounds tractive effort— approximately 40 percent more than the Challengers. A Big Boy could easily lift a 120-car freight train over the 0.82 percent grades on Sherman Hill and were rated to haul up to 8,000 tons unassisted on level track.

Despite their spectacular performance, the Big Boy was not a popular type and remained unique to Union Pacific. Initially, the railroad ordered 20 Big Boys from Alco, and the first was delivered in September 1941 on the eve of America's involvement in World War II. This was an especially timely delivery, as the war would dramatically increase the volume of traffic moving over American rails. To help cope with this tremendous increase in business, UP ordered another five Big Boys from Alco in 1943. They were delivered in 1944 and were marginally heavier than the first 20, primarily because of wartime restrictions on alloyed steel.

The Big Boys were among the last large steam locomotives operating in the U.S. and handled seasonal rush traffic through the 1950s. Because of this late-era performance, their operation is well-remembered and adequately documented on film. Of the 25 Big Boys built, eight were preserved and are displayed all around the country including at Cheyenne, Denver, Los Angeles, and Scranton, Pennsylvania. Although there are no operating Big Boys, there has been talk of restoring one.

For most U.S. railroads, their first diesels were switchers; but Union Pacific's first diesel-electric was the high-speed power car on the M-10001 *City of Portland* streamliner, shown on exhibition at an unidentified location circa 1935. Working with Pullman Car & Manufacturing Company, Electro-Motive assembled the power car and delivered it with a 900-hp. 201-A engine built by GM subsidiary and Electro-Motive affiliate Winton Engine Company. This was the first V-type engine block to be used in American rail passenger service. However, within a short period, the train was returned to Electro-Motive and Pullman for modifications, and the power plant was replaced by a 1,200-hp. Winton engine. *Otto C. Perry, Denver Public Library, Western History Department*

The Changing of the Guard

DIESELS TAKE OVER FROM STEAM

U nion Pacific was one of the early developers and pioneer users of internal-combustion power. As early as 1904, UP was examining the potential of internal-combustion power and eventually operated a number of motor-powered railcars that could be considered precursors to the diesel-electric locomotive. UP's first diesel would arrive in 1934, long before most other railroads were even thinking of diesel power.

PASSENGER DIESELS

Electro-Motive

UP's first true diesel-electric was the power car for the M-10001 streamliner set delivered in 1934 and launched in 1935 as the *City of Portland* streamliner. Only months earlier, the railroad had debuted its first streamliner, the M-10000, but that housed a distillate engine that was but a distant cousin of a diesel-electric power plant. Distillate fuel required an external spark for ignition rather than relying on compression as required by a diesel engine. The subsequent articulated streamliners employed Winton 201 diesel engines. All the M-series streamliners that followed the M-10000 were diesel-electric powered using Electro-Motive's 201-A power plant supplied by subsidiary Winton Engine Company. For additional information on the M-series streamliners, see chapter 5.

The power cars for the early M-series streamliners were more or less integral to their trainsets. By 1936 Union Pacific had learned that separate locomotives and interchangeable passenger cars were better-suited for its passenger service than inflexible semi-permanently coupled articulated train sets, so it ordered some of Electro-Motive's first streamlined diesel-electric locomotives and conventionally coupled streamlined passenger cars. Two sets of A-B-B (a cabbed unit and two cabless boosters) E2s were built for the *City of San Francisco* and *City of Los Angeles* and numbered SF-1,-2,-3 and LA-1,-2,-3 respectively. The E2 model featured two 900 hp. Winton engines, producing a total output of 1,800 hp. Electro-Motive's "E"-series designation stems from the output of these early passenger diesels ("Eighteen hundred"). All E-units rode on a pair of "A-1-A" trucks, whereby each truck had three wheelsets, with the center axle/wheelset unpowered and used for more even weight distribution.

The E2s featured a noticeably different streamlining treatment than all other E-series models in that the nose was more bulbous and swooped back toward the pilot rather than sloped forward (see pages 82–83). In addition there were groups of three porthole windows on the sides of the locomotive. Both sets carried a brilliant chrome shield on the front of the cab unit that featured the emblems of the railroads that operated each of these trains.

As UP expanded its streamliner fleet, adding new sets of equipment and additional routes, it purchased more Electro-Motive E-units. Prior to World War II, UP acquired E3s and E6s, both rated at 2,000 hp. Initially these locomotives operated in dedicated service on a specific train and were lettered accordingly (again, see pages 82–83). After the war, UP bought large numbers of E7s, E8s, and E9s, rated at 2,000, 2,250, and 2,400 hp. respectively. By this time the E-units were operated in a passenger pool and no longer painted for specific trains. UP continued to purchase E-units

for another two decades. It was among the last railroads to buy traditional passenger power from Electro-Motive and bought its last E9s in 1964, years after most American railroads had bought their last passenger diesels.

Unlike many Western lines that used variations on the four-axle F-unit to haul their fancy limiteds, UP preferred six-axle passenger locomotives. The Western Pacific, Northern Pacific, and Denver & Rio Grande Western never owned any Es, and Santa Fe, which owned just a few, was better known for its fleet of Fs. But, Union Pacific also had a small fleet of passenger F3s—five A-units, and one B, all built in 1947 and rated at 1,500 hp.—and a pair of FP7s. The four-axle F-unit had a tractive effort advantage over the E-unit because all of the locomotive weight was on driving wheels. The F3s were used to haul conventional heavyweight trains such as the *Overland Limited* over the heavily graded lines in Wyoming.

American Locomotive Company (Alco)

Compared the large numbers of Electro-Motive E-units, the Alco PA/PB passenger locomotive was a short-lived and obscure motive-power aberration on the Union Pacific. Where the E-unit in its various forms had more than a 35-year run in regular passenger service and has survived into modern times for use on excursion trains and business-train specials, the Alco PA survived for less than a decade in UP passenger service. UP bought two orders of Alco passenger cabs, the first in 1947 and the second in 1949. They were rated at 2,000 hp. When these locomotives were constructed, the PA/PB designation had not yet been adopted and was applied retroactively to UP's locomotives. As passenger locomotives, the cabs produced 59,490 pounds of tractive effort and the boosters slightly less.

The Alco PA's performance was not as good as the Es, and the Alcos were not highly regarded by the railroad. The PA's strength was on mountainous lines, and so UP primarily assigned them to secondary runs between Cheyenne and Los Angeles. They were regular power on the LA&SL in the late 1940s and early 1950s, and often worked the *Utahn, Los Angeles Limited, Pony Express,* and *Pacific Limited.*

In 1955 Union Pacific re-geared its PA/PBs for pulling power rather than speed and assigned them to freight service, making UP one of a only a few lines to regularly use PAs on freight. They were typically assigned to work in Nebraska and Kansas. One PA was rebuilt in the late 1950s for use as a cab for an experimental coal-fired gas turbine.

Fairbanks-Morse

Union Pacific operated the largest fleet of Fairbanks-Morse "Erie-Built" diesels in the West. The first order was delivered in December 1945. These were rated at 2,000 hp. each and typically used in sets of three. Initially they used a 68:19 gear ratio intended for a

maximum 75 mph operation and assigned to heavy freight service. According to William Kratville in his *Motive Power on the Union Pacific*, one 6,000-hp. set hauled a 62-car freight weighing 3,100 tons west out of Council Bluffs in a celebrated test run. The F-M's did not perform satisfactorily as freight locomotives and in May 1946 UP regeared them with a 63:24 gear ratio, which allowed them to operate up to 102 mph, and assigned them to passenger service on the Los Angeles & Salt Lake. Initially they were assigned to the premier *City of Los Angeles* but did not hold this run long and were soon assigned to secondary passenger trains along with the Alco PA/PBs.

Additional Eries were delivered in 1947 and 1948, giving UP a total of 13 of this model. In 1955 all were regeared with a 68:19 ratio and again assigned to freight service. All were disposed of in the early 1960s.

Freight Power and Diesel Switchers

Freight service has always been Union Pacific's first concern, and freight locomotives have long represented the majority of its fleet. Although UP was quick to adopt internal-combustion power for passenger work and began to sample diesel switchers in the late 1930s, the railroad was hesitant to purchase diesels for over-the-road freight work and did not acquire road freight locomotives until after World War II. Unlike competitors Santa Fe and Chicago, Burlington & Quincy, UP was

unimpressed by Electro-Motive's pioneering FT freight diesel of 1939 and elected to stay with steam technology rather than purchase FT sets. Santa Fe was quick to take advantage of the FT on its arid lines in the Southwest, but UP went on to design its famous Big Boy and ordered dozens of new steam locomotives in the early 1940s for both heavy freight and passenger work.

Finally, after the war had ended, UP recognized the advantages of diesel power and ordered road freight locomotives from F-M (see above), Alco, and EMD. Yet, UP overall was slow to dieselize and continued to rely on steam power until the late 1950s. Even after

An A-B-A set of Alco PAs speed along the old Kansas Pacific main with the first section of the *Pony Express* circa 1950. *Otto C. Perry, Denver Public Library, Western History Department*

UP sampled Alco's FA/FB freight cab locomotives, one of which rides the turntable at Ogden in 1957. *John Dziobko* the diesel's cost advantage over steam had been clearly demonstrated, the railroad remained unsure about the diesel. So even after it had hundreds of diesels working in freight service, UP looked to the gas-turbine to produce the greater power it needed. Ultimately, the diesel won out and today UP's entire locomotive fleet, save for its two historic steam locomotives, is comprised of diesels.

Fairbanks-Morse

In the 1930s, Fairbanks-Morse developed a two-cycle opposed-piston engine for Navy submarines. An opposed-piston engine has two cylinders facing one another within each cylinder. The design has several potential advantages over conventional diesel engine designs. It requires fewer moving parts, enjoys superior heat dissipation, operates at a lower piston speed, and involves a simpler overall design. By 1940, F-M was the second largest diesel engine manufacturer in the U.S. and

was supplying engines for submarines and other military applications. In 1943, F-M recognized that, although its business was booming because of wartime demand, it needed to find civilian markets for its engines if it were to survive a postwar environment. By mid-1944, F-M had entered the heavy locomotive business, with locomotive designs based on variations of its successful 38D8-1/8 opposed-piston engine. The OP engine performed well in marine applications, but in the railroad environment they were loners in a world of diesel technology heavily weighted toward traditional piston-engine design. A few railroads—notably the Milwaukee Road—embraced F-M locomotives, operat-.ing them successfully for decades, but for UP its F-Ms were troublesome.

As discussed earlier, UP acquired Fairbanks-Morse dual-purpose Erie-Builts primarily for freight service. Although these were later assigned to passenger duties, they can be considered UP's first road freight diesels. UP also acquired a small fleet of F-M switchers and road-switchers, the most powerful of which were 10 H20-44s built in 1947. Many of these locomotives worked as helpers over Cajon Pass in Southern California. UP had five F-M H10-44 switchers. It also operated five H15-44s purchased in 1948 and three H16-44s purchased in 1950 These produced 1,500 and 1,600 hp. respectively. Some of UP's F-M road-switchers were traded to Electro-Motive in the late 1960s for SD45s.

Alco

Alco had been Union Pacific's primary locomotive producer in the late steam era. It had built UP's fleet of 4-12-2s, its famous 800-series 4-8-4s, 4-6-6-4 Challengers, and massive 4-8-8-4 Big Boys. Unfortunately for Alco, it would not fair so well with UP in the diesel era.

UP bought 100 switchers from Alco; 54, World War II-era S-2s, a sole S-3, and 45 S-4s built in the mid-1950s. Although fairly numerous, these utilitarian workhorses, like Alco switchers all over the nation, worked a host of vital, but

An Alco S-series switcher pulls the *City of Denver/City of Portland* backward into Denver Union Station on a spring day in 1967.
Ron Lundstrom

Alco RS1s delivered for use on UP subsidiary Spokane International in 1949 wore Armour yellow and gray. SI 1222 is shown in 1969 at Omaha. *Mike Schafer*

Among the more rare diesel types purchased by UP were ten Alco RSC2s. Delivered in the late 1940s, these locomotives were intended for branchline duties. Three-axle trucks were used to more evenly distribute weight on light branchline track. *Mike McBride*

low-profile assignments. They switched coach yards, scavenged alleyways and obscure side tracks for freight cars in industrial districts, and drilled in yards large and small all around the railroad. A few were built for multiple-unit operation an assigned branchline work.

UP's first and largest fleet of Alco road diesels were 88 FA/FB road freight units purchased between 1947 and 1948. They were rated at 1,500 hp., featured a 74:18 gear ratio, and used a 12-cylinder 244 diesel engine. A number of FA/FBs were originally often assigned to work on the LA&SL along with EMD F3s. Despite its allegiance to steam and its reluctance to dieselize its Wyoming operations, UP looked to the diesel to solve some of

its operational headaches on the heavily graded, dry, LA&SL route. Diesels offered a simple solution to UP's complex helper arrangements; they were sufficiently powerful to handle heavy freights unassisted and effectively eliminated the need for helpers on most LA&SL grades. As a result the LA&SL was effectively dieselized by 1948, more than a decade early than other areas of the railroad. However, the Alcos were short-lived, as they had difficulties with standing the rigors of the harsh desert environment. They were eventually reassigned to the relative flat areas east of North Platte.

UP also purchased 16 Alco road-switchers in 1947 and 1948, 6 RS2s with B-B (four-motor, four-axle) trucks, and 10 RSC2s with A-1-A (four-motor, six-axle) trucks. Both were rated at 1,500 hp. UP's RSC2s were an especially unusual model; only 87 were built total, and just 15 were built to the specifications that UP used. The RSC2 distributed its weight over six-axles for lighter axle loadings and was typically assigned to lightweight branch lines where locomotives with heavier axle loadings were prohibited.

UP acquired 13 RS1s for subsidiary Spokane International in 1958. These were built in 1949, used a 75:16 gear ratio, 40-inch wheels, and delivered 1,000 hp.

Union Pacific shied away from Alco products in the 1950s and 1960s, tending to favor EMD and General Electric locomotives instead. However, in the early 1960s UP acquired four Alco RS27 demonstrators—four-axle road-switchers rated at 2,400 hp. UP sampled Alco's 8-axle Century 855s (sidebar) and purchased 10 C630s in 1966. The latter were six-axle, six-motor locomotives rated at 3,000 hp. The model was designed to compete with Electro-Motive's SD40 and GE's U30C, but the Alcos proved less reliable than these other, more popular models and did not last long on the UP.

Baldwin

Union Pacific was not a large purchaser of Baldwin diesels. It operated a handful of Baldwin VO1000 switchers which were built in 1943 and dressed in black paint with yellow lettering and red and yellow "Road of the Challengers" slogans on the cab. These were primarily assigned to Council Bluffs. UP also had a sole DRS6-4-1500 road-switcher that featured A-1-A trucks, and six AS616 road-switchers with C-C (three-axle, three-motor) trucks.

Union Pacific's most intriguing order from Baldwin were a pair of DR12-8-1500/2SC "Centipedes" to be numbered 998 and 999, described in John Kirkland's *The Diesel Builders*, Volume III. These curious machines, constructed in 1948, used 24 wheels in a 2-D+D-2 arrangement and produced 3,000 hp. each. However, before they were delivered, UP cancelled the order. They were essentially the same as the Centipedes built for Seaboard, Pennsylvania, and National Railways of Mexico and had a short career working as Baldwin demonstrators before being sent for scrap.

Electro-Motive

In October 1939, UP acquired its first Electro-Motive switchers. These gave a successful

In the Columbia River Gorge in the 1950s, a classic A-B-A (cab-booster-cab) set of F7s have freight in tow. Electro-Motive F-units were the mainstay of diesel road-freight power on U.S. railroads in the postwar era, although UP's F-unit fleet was relatively small. *UP, Dave Oroszi collection*

performance, and the railroad purchased more during the next 14 years, amassing a fair roster of NW2s, SW7s, SW9s and SW1200s. In 1951 UP purchased eight TR5 two-unit "cow-and-calf" transfer switcher sets that were rated at 2,400 hp. and delivered 123,680 pounds of tractive effort.

In May 1947 UP received the first its EMD road freight locomotive, F3A No. 1400. The F3s were very successful, and several orders of F3s were delivered between 1947 and 1949. They were rated at 1,500 hp. though some were later upgraded to more modern F7 or F9 specifications. A number of UP's F3s were equipped with large homebuilt plows for service in the Pacific Northwest. In 1951, EMD built a small fleet of F7s to augment UP's F3 fleet. While UP operated roughly 150 F-units, its fleet was relatively small compared to the enormous numbers of Fs used elsewhere around the U.S.

In 1953, EMD built 30 GP7 road-switchers for UP. Like the F3s and F7s, these were rated at 1,500 hp. The GP's versatility and reliability made it the most popular locomotive in America, and UP ordered hundreds more "Geeps" (pronounced "jeeps") from EMD between 1954 and 1957. These were the

slightly more powerful (and seemingly ubiquitous) GP9. UP along with the Pennsylvania Railroad ordered cabless GP9Bs. Union Pacific wanted to obtain more power from its GP9s than the 1,750 hp. offered by their 567C prime mover, so it rebuilt some of its Geeps with turbochargers at its Omaha Shops. These locomotives are colloquially known as "Omaha GP20s." UP's modification proved successful and encouraged Electro-Motive to develop its own turbocharged models. EMD had traditionally relied on its traditional Roots blower to aspirate all of its locomotive engines, but the turbocharger proved the most economical way to obtain significantly greater power from the aged 567 engine design. Following UP's lead, EMD developed the 567D2 engine for its new GP20, and SD24 models. UP responded by sending additional GP9s back to EMD for conversion to GP20 specifications and was one of the largest buyers of the SD24.

Union Pacific painted its road-switchers in its attractive Armour yellow and gray paint, accented with red stripes and catchy slogans on the sides. Some featured "Serves All the West" in large block letters below the windows on the cab, while others read "Road of the Streamliners" in fancy stylized script.

UP was an early buyer of EMD six-axle locomotives and bought 10 1,500-hp SD7s in 1953. Although it did not express any interest in the more popular SD9, UP was a large buyer of the turbocharged SD24, rated at 2,400 hp., and bought both cab and cabless versions. The SD24s were mostly assigned to the LA&SL and spent most of their careers hauling long freights across the desert mountains between Salt Lake City and Los Angeles. These pioneering turbocharged EMDs were considered powerful for their time but were not as reliable as later EMD models and consequentially did not last as long as more successful models. UP seriously considered rebuilding its SD24 fleet, and in July 1968 rebuilt one locomotive with a 16-cylinder 645E prime mover, the engine-type used in EMD's highly successful SD40 locomotive. According to the *Contemporary Diesel Spotters Guide*, this locomotive—which variously held the number 99, 3100, 3200, 3399 and 3999— was rated at 3,300 hp. and was used as a test bed for a constant-speed engine. Another SD24, No. 414, was rebuilt in 1975, with an updated electrical system, but retaining the 567D prime mover.

Second-Generation EMD

The advent of the turbocharger resulted in a whole new line of EMD locomotives. The GP20 and SD24 are generally considered transitional locomotives that share characteristics with both first-generation and second-generation locomotives. In the early 1960s, UP bought large numbers of EMD's new, more-powerful locomotives. In 1962 and 1963 more than 100 GP30s arrived from EMD. These locomotives featured a distinctive bulge above the cab. The GP30 produced 2,250 hp. using a 567D3 prime mover. UP also acquired a fleet of cabless GP30Bs. As with the SD24Bs, UP was the only line to acquire this unusual model.

In 1964, UP took delivery of 24 2,500 hp. GP35s. These high-horsepower, four-axle locomotives were designed for fast freight service, but they were plagued with reliability problems stemming from their turbocharged 567-series engine. As a result, many were later rebuilt for local work.

Electro-Motive acknowledged that it needed a new engine design and in 1965 it introduced a new generation of prime mover that overcame flaws exhibited by turbocharged 567 engines. This was the 645 engine, which represented a refinement and enlargement of the 567 design. (The cylinder bore was increased from 567 cubic inches to 645 cubic inches—thus the new designation). The new engine coincided with the introduction of a whole new line of locomotives that also employed an entirely new AC-DC electrical system which used an alternator in the place of a generator and employed silicon diodes to rectify the alternating current to direct current for the traction motors. This development reduced the number of electrical parts, decreased maintenance, and—more importantly—provided a significantly higher output to the traction motors.

One of these new models was the SD40, a 3,000 hp., six-axle, six-motor locomotive. UP was especially taken with this model and by 1971 had taken delivery of more than 120 of them. UP also bought 50 EMD SD45s, which used a 20-cylinder 645E3 engine to generate

3,600 hp. Based on UP's record for demanding ever greater power, it would have seemed logical for UP to have purchased a greater quantity of SD45s than it did. This model proved very popular with the other Western lines, especially Southern Pacific and Santa Fe, but difficulties with the 20-cylinder engine crankshaft and high fuel consumption, plus UP's interest in the super powerful, eight-axle DDA40X (sidebar) discouraged additional SD45 purchases.

THE STANDARDIZATION DIESEL ERA

In the early 1970s Union Pacific adopted a new motive-power philosophy. Instead of ordering specially-built high-horsepower locomotives such as its gas-turbines and eight-axle diesels and a colorful potpourri of commercially offered diesel types, which had typified its locomotive purchases since the mid 1940s, it focused the majority of its new locomotive acquisitions on standard 3,000-hp., six-axle, six-motor models. This horsepower range and

motor/axled format have proven the most versatile and the most reliable.

Although UP purchased a large number of GE U30Cs and C30-7s, the largest number of new locomotives were more than 600 SD40–2s acquired between 1972 and 1982. Within a fairly short span of time, the SD40–2 became the most common locomotive on the Union Pacific. These powerful, reliable locomotives were used in all types of freight service. They led long drags, hauled coal trains, worked in local and yard service, served as helper sets, and sprinted across the plains and deserts with intermodal trains. In the mid-1970s UP equipped roughly 90 of its SD40–2s with a gear ratio for 83 mph operation for work in fast freight service. Other SD40–2s were equipped for radio-control helper service and had extended short hoods to accommodate the radio equipment. For two decades, UP SD40–2s were to be found nearly everywhere in the West and were typically ignored by

Mainstay road-freight diesels on the UP for many years was Electro-Motive's popular SD40/SD40–2 model. Three SD40–2s make easy work of an eastbound freight at Hermosa, Wyoming, in 1993. *John Leopard*

SD60M No. 6104 wheeling through western Nebraska in 1989 illustrates the wide-nose safety cabs—or "comfort cabs"—introduced on many new locomotives in the 1980s. Early versions of this diesel type, as evident on the 6104, had three-piece windshields. *Brian Solomon*

enthusiasts because of their ubiquitous presence. As this was being written in 1999, the SD40–2 still had an active roll on UP main lines, although newer, more technologically sophisticated and more-powerful locomotives have long since claimed the premier runs. Many SD40–2s were later converted to ersatz B-units by removing some cab controls. These locomotives were designated SD40–2B.

In February 1986, EMD began delivering its new SD60 to Union Pacific. This 3,800-hp. locomotive employed the new 16-cylinder 710G engine, an improved design based on an enlargement of the older 645 engine; the stroke was increased from 9^1/$_{16}$ inches to 11 inches. UP had 88 SD60s by June 1988 .

In the mid 1980s, Union Pacific and Santa Fe both approached EMD about building locomotives with "wide nose" safety cabs, also known as "comfort cabs." UP was the first railroad in the U.S. to acquire locomotives employing this new style of cab, which was an adaptation of the Canadian Cab. It received an order of SD60Ms beginning in January 1989. The early SD60M style featured a three-piece windshield, while later locomotives used a

two-piece windshield. GE responded, and in 1990 UP acquired its first six-axle GEs with safety cabs. The safety cab has since become a standard feature, and today most new locomotives for U.S. service are so equipped.

Union Pacific has had a long relationship with General Electric, and has been using GE locomotives for more than six decades. Years before GE began producing its own diesel-electric locomotives in competition General Motors' Electro-Motive Division and its one-time business partner Alco, UP had purchased GE turbines (sidebar). In 1947 Union Pacific acquired its first GE diesel, a 44-ton switcher. This lone unit was tested at yards around the system and eventually was assigned as the shop switcher at Pocatello. It was painted in Armour yellow and gray with red striping and lettering, like UP's road locomotives.

GE's formal break with Alco in 1953 was the first step toward developing its own heavy road locomotive line. In 1954, GE built a 6,000-hp., four-unit, full-carbody locomotive powered by Cooper-Bessemer four-cycle diesel engines. Two units of the four-unit set—which was designated as an XP24-1—were rated at 1,200 hp. and two at 1,800 hp. This locomotive was promoted as an export locomotive test bed and tested on the Erie Railroad, in Erie paint. UP later acquired the XP24-1 and dressed it in UP paint.

Based on its experience with prototypes and export locomotives, in 1960 GE debuted its 2,500 hp. U25B for domestic applications. UP was one of GEs first U25B customers and bought a total of 16, including four high-hood demonstrators. These were followed by a fleet of U50s (sidebar) and a variety of six-motor models consisting of ten 2,800-hp. U28Cs in 1966, 150 3,000-hp. U30C's acquired between 1972 and 1976, and 140 3,000-hp. C30-7s acquired between 1977 and 1981.

GE's Universal Line and the subsequent DASH 7 line performed reasonably well but suffered from reliability problems that limited sales and resulted in shorter service lives than comparable EMD locomotives. During the mid 1980s, GE made a concerted effort to improve its product in order to capture greater market share and introduced it DASH 8 line. The Dash 8's superior performance and reliability gave GE an edge over EMD, allowing GE to ascend to the role as America's premier locomotive manufacturer.

Union Pacific supported GE by purchasing 60 C36–7s, a transitional model rated at 3,600 hp., and then in the late 1980s and early 1990s it bought 256 DASH 8–40Cs (UP designation C40–8), followed by 50 DASH 8–40CWs (the first GE locomotives equipped with safety cabs, which UP designates C40–8W), and 154 DASH 8–41CW. UP has become one of GE's largest customers and has continued to acquire large numbers of GE locomotives through the 1990s. In the summer of 1994, UP received 40 DASH 9-44CWs, (UP designation (C44–9W), 4,400-hp. locomotives equipped with safety cabs that incorporated several improved features including split cooling and GE's high-adhesion trucks.

AC POWER

In the mid 1990s, both GM and GE began building diesel-electric locomotives with alternating current (AC) traction motors instead of conventional direct current motors. These locomotives exhibit a number of advantages—mainly increased tractive effort and superior dynamic braking—that has made them especially desirable for heavy freight service, especially coal work. The first generation of AC traction locomotives did not appear significantly different than their conventional DC counterparts. Although UP was not the first railroad to employ a large fleet of ACs, it has become one of the largest users of this evolutionary new technology.

UP received it first AC locomotive, a GE AC4400CW (which UP designates as a C44AC) in October 1994, part of an order of three AC locomotives from GE. UP ordered another 150 GE AC4400CWs which began arriving in March 1996, by which time the railroad had inherited Chicago & North Western's fleet of AC4400CW's through merger.

DISTRIBUTED POWER

In 1995, UP reintroduced, unmanned radio-controlled remote helpers, known in modern terminology as Distributed Power Units (DPUs). A number of GE AC4400CWs were equipped with Locotrol III technology, a vastly improved radio remote system, enabling a locomotive engineer to control up to four separate sets of locomotives—although UP typically only operates two or three sets. After a few break-in difficulties were worked out, Union Pacific enjoyed considerable success employing the new technology, and today DPUs are regularly used in a variety of applications around the system.

6,000-HP. ACS

In the mid-1990s, both GE and General Motors (EMD and General Motors Limited in Canada) began developing single-unit, single-engine, 6,000-hp. locomotives using AC traction technology. UP was the first railroad to order 6,000-hp. locomotives and, as of this writing, was the only line to order 6,000-hp. units from both builders.

In order to develop this extraordinary output from a single diesel prime mover, both GE and GM resorted to developing new engine designs. Since these new engines were not ready for regular production at a time when UP had a high demand for new locomotives, both manufacturers built "convertible" or "upgradeable" designs built with older, lower horsepower engines, but capable of accepting the new, more-powerful engines when they became available. Between December 1995 and September 1997 Union Pacific received 70 GEs designated C6044ACs and 170 GMs designated SD9043MACs. These unorthodox designations reflect the engine upgrade feature. By 1998 both manufactures were building their new engines.

UP's Big Double Diesels

"Double diesel" Centennial 6941dwarfs its companion locomotives on a westbound freight drifting down the west slope of Sherman Hill east of Laramie, Wyoming, in 1980. *Steve Smedley*

Union Pacific was long known for its interest in large, super-powerful locomotives. Its 4-12-2s were the largest non-articulated steam when they were new in 1926. The Big Boy was known as the world's largest steam locomotive (never mind that C&O's 2-6-6-6 was larger). UP's gas-turbines redefined big in the 1950s. In the early 1960s, UP was looking for big diesels, bigger than had ever been built before. The reason was simple: big diesels reduced the need for large, unwieldy locomotive consists.

Without developing any revolutionary technology, all three builders in the early 1960s fulfilled the letter of UP's power lust, if not entirely in the spirit of its need for power.

General Electric's Entries

GE pioneered the eight-axle, dual-engine, diesel-electric locomotive. GE's monstrous double-diesels were introduced in late 1963 and designated U50 (Universal Line, 5,000 hp.). Powered by a pair of FDL-16 diesel engines, they rode on an unorthodox B-B+B-B wheel arrangement. The locomotives measured 85 feet 6.5 inches long and were in essence two GE U25Bs riding a single frame. The trucks were salvaged from retired turbine locomotives.

UP took delivery of 23 U50s in 1965 (SP also bought U50s). In 1969, UP ordered a fleet of 46 similar locomotives, designated U50C, that used 12-cylinder FDL engines and C-C trucks salvaged from the 8,500-hp. turbines.

Electro-Motive's Double Diesels

Following GE's lead, Electro-Motive produced the dual-engine DD35 that was essentially two GP35s in one carbody. It used two turbocharged, 16-cylinder 567D3A engines on an 88-foot, 2-inch-long, non-articulated frame and rode on a pair of four-axle "D" trucks with a 17-foot, 1.5-inch wheel base—the longest of any diesel-electric locomotive in America. The DD35 produced 5,000 hp.—exactly the rated output of a pair of GP35s. Although EMD intended the locomotive as a high-horsepower booster only, on request of UP, the DD35 was later offered in both cab and booster configurations. The B-units were introduced first and were built in 1963–64; the A-units were built in 1965. UP bought most of the production, acquiring 42 DD35s (15 DD35As and 27 DD35Bs).

Electro-Motive considered expanding the DD35 concept into a DD40A that would have been powered by dual 16-cylinder 645s and rated at 6,000 hp—essentially two GP40s under one hood. The intended customer would have been Union Pacific, but none were sold.

The largest locomotive of the era was the gargantuan double-engine DDA40X built for UP beginning in 1969. They were known as Centennials and numbered in the 6900 series to commemorate the 100th anniversary of the completion of the transcontinental railway. True to Union Pacific nature, the DDA40X locomotives were—and are— indeed

Two pondering General Electric U50Cs and a GE U28C lumber out of Kearney, Nebraska, with a westbound freight in the spring of 1971. Standing in the background are an EMD GP30 and an early high-nose GE U25B. *Mike Schafer*

the largest and most-powerful single-unit diesel-electrics in the world.

The DDA40X stretched out to 98 feet 5 inches, more than 10 feet longer than the DD35A, and like the DD35 used a 17-foot, 1.5-inch wheel base. It was powered by a pair of 16-cylinder 645E engines that generated 6,600 hp. UP took delivery of 47 Centennials between April 1969 and September 1971. They worked the transcontinental routes for a decade and were common power on the LA&SL route before being stored because of the recession in the early 1980s. In 1984, traffic picked up, and the Centennials had one last blast before being retired. By this time, UP had purchased the Western Pacific, and the Centennials were making regular forays into Northern California via the famous Feather River Canyon.

Several UP Centennials have been preserved, including No. 6936 by UP, which keeps it in running order as part of its Historic Fleet. This locomotive makes occasional appearances on excursion trains, but has also been pressed into freight service from time to time when traffic demands it.

Incredible Hulks: Alco's Big Centurys

In June 1964, Alco constructed an A-B-A set of eight-axle Century 855s for UP. Each locomotive was powered by a pair of 16-cylinder, 251C diesel engines which produced 2,750 hp. The individual locomotives were rated at 5,500 hp. each—slightly higher than GE's and EMD's big double diesels—and the whole trio generated a phenomenal 16,500 hp. Each locomotive was 83 feet, 11 inches long, weighed 528,000 pounds, and rode on four sets of four-axle trucks similar to GE's U50. These gargantuan locomotives did not fair well compared to the other double-diesels and were scrapped by the end of the decade.

Epilogue

UP's exploration of the double diesel was expensive and relatively short-lived. By 1971, it had ordered its last double diesel, just eight years after it acquired its first. From that point on it chose to purchase more versatile, conventional diesel models and began acquiring them in great numbers in the early 1970s.

Among the most monstrous diesel types ever acquired by UP were its three Alco Century 855s delivered in 1964. They tended to gravitate to Omaha since they needed the constant attention of shop forces. All three units—the only three of this model ever built—were scrapped in 1971. *UP, Dave Oroszi collection*

Three GE C36–7s pilot an auto-rack train over former-Missouri Pacific trackage at Knob Noster, Missouri, in July 1990. These units were part of a 1985 delivery of 60 C36–7s to Missouri Pacific, then on the cusp of merger with UP. *F. L. Becht*

MODERN MERGER ACQUISITIONS

During the 1980s and 1990s UP's diesel fleet swelled with locomotives acquired through mergers. As the UP grew to include the Missouri Pacific, Western Pacific, Katy, Chicago & North Western, and Southern Pacific/Rio Grande, it inherited great variety of locomotive types that it had not previously owned in addition to numerous models it already had on its roster. Furthermore, some locomotive types that UP had retired years earlier were on the books again. Among new models, MP brought EMD's GP15, GP15AC, GP18, GP38, GP38–2, GP50, SD50, SW1500, MP15DC, and GE's B23–7 and B30–7A models; meanwhile, Western Pacific added the SW1500, GE U23B, and U30B models. Katy's rag-tag roster contained few factory-new locomotives in 1988, but it contributed some types unfamiliar to the "classic Union Pacific," including EMD's MP15AC, GP38AC, and GP39 models, plus a slug rebuilt from an F-unit and a modified F-unit cab converted to B-unit status with GP38 specifications, designated F38B; it also received six mongrel "RS3Ms" remanufactured from Alco RS3s with EMD 16-567C engines. According to Don Strack's *Union Pacific Locomotive Directory 1998*, the absorption of C&NW in 1995 added 776 locomotives to the UP roster, including many models that UP was already operating. Most useful to UP was C&NW's fleet of nearly new GE DASH–9s, AC4400CWs, and slightly older DASH8–40Cs and SD60s—models UP had also recently acquired new. However, with these newer locomotives came a collection of rolling antiques, including some 90 40-year-old GP7s (which had been rebuilt as GP7Rs), a number of which had been built for the late, lamented Rock Island; 16 GP9Rs, 23 SD18Rs (rebuilt from SD24s), 13 SD45s and a lone SD45R. Most of these worn-out locomotives were disposed within a year or two of the merger. C&NW also provided a fair number of GP15–1, GP38–2, GP40, GP50, SD40–2, and SD50 models. New models to UP with the C&NW were 10 SD38–2s, another SD45R, and an unusual locomotive powered by a 12-cylinder Caterpillar diesel, designated SDCAT. Neither of these two locomotives were assigned UP numbers. Four C&NW F7As and three F7Bs were added to the UPs historic fleet and sent to Cheyenne.

UP's merger with SP in 1996 added 2,376 locomotives, according to Strack, and introduced a variety of new types to UP's roster, along with many familiar locomotives that have been assimilated into UP's existing fleet. At the time of the merger, some SP locomotives still wore Rio Grande paint predating the SP and Rio Grande amalgamation in 1988. In addition, a large number of SP's fleet were lettered for its Cotton Belt subsidiary.

Southern Pacific had pioneered the SD45T–2 and SD40T–2 Tunnel Motor types to achieve better performance on its heavily tunneled lines in the Sierra and Cascades. Most of these locomotives had been rebuilt during the 1980s, and many joined UP's fleet at the time of the merger. Among the new models that SP added to UP's fleet were EMD GP60s, SD39s, SD70Ms, and GE B30–7s, B36–7s, B39–8s and DASH8–40Bs. SP had also acquired a large fleet of DASH 9s and AC4400CWs between 1994 and 1996, which fit in well to UP's motive-power scheme. Among the antiques, UP found itself with SP SD9Es, GP35Es, and a handful of Rio Grande GP30s which were largely kept in former Rio Grande territory making for an unlikely contrast to the modern Union Pacific image.

Many of the inherited locomotives were renumbered and painted in UP's handsome Armour yellow while others were disposed of without ever carrying UP identification. For a few years after the merger with MP, some of that line's locomotives continued to carry Missouri Pacific lettering while wearing UP paint. At least one Western Pacific locomotive was also given this treatment. As this is being written at the close of 1999, many locomotives are still roving the Union Pacific system wearing C&NW, SP, Cotton Belt, and Rio Grande paint, making for an uncharacteristically colorful fleet. It is anticipated that spectral homogeny will soon return to UP as inherited locomotives are either painted or purged.

An Electro-Motive SD90MAC heads up a westbound freight on the former Chicago & North Western main line at Nelson, Illinois, in 1999. The coaling tower at this junction point between the Chicago–Omaha main and the St. Louis line stands as a reminder of the steam era. *Dan Montague*

Union Pacific's longtime experimentation with turbine locomotives was in its waning years as GE gas-turbine set No. 7 (along with one of UP's massive Alco C855s) howl upgrade out of Omaha with a westbound train in the summer of 1965. These final gas-turbines represented some serious locomotive technology—they could develop an astounding 8,500 hp., or more under ideal conditions. *Ron Lundstrom*

The Turbines

UP'S REMARKABLE FLEET OF TURBINE-TYPE MOTIVE POWER

Union Pacific has had the most extensive and the most diverse experience using turbine-powered freight locomotives in the world. Beginning in the late 1930s and for more than three decades, it experimented with various types of turbines and was the only American railroad to operate a significant turbine fleet in freight service.

General Electric, one of the world's foremost designers of turbine engines, built an experimental, two-unit, oil-fired steam-turbine-electric locomotive for Union Pacific in 1938. This extremely powerful locomotive was unlike anything ever built before and displayed a number of impressive characteristics. Externally it featured an impressive streamlined body with a long bulbous cab nose that resembled UP's later diesel-powered streamliners. To the untrained observer, this locomotive might be mistaken for a diesel-electric. Although it used an electric drive, it was really a steam locomotive, and some experts consider it to be one of the most advanced designs ever built in the history of steam. UP historian Alfred Bruce describes it as ". . . one of the most exceptional steam locomotives ever built and should be recognized as a pioneer because of its conception, design, and construction."

Each locomotive employed an extremely high-pressure water-tube boiler that worked at 1,500 psi and superheated steam to 920 degrees Fahrenheit (typical modern reciprocating steam locomotive boilers worked at just 250–300 psi). Each locomotive delivered 2,500 hp. for a total of 5,000 hp. for the pair. Each of the two units had four sets of trucks in 2-C+C-2 arrangement (described by Bruce in steam terminology as a 4-6-0–0-6-4T wheel arrangement, giving the entire two-engine arrangement a preposterous 4-6-0/0-6-4T+4-6-0/0-6-4T

arrangement!) The locomotive was designed to attain speeds up to 125 mph. Together the two units weighed over a million pounds and placed 708,000 pounds on the driving wheels. Although promoted as a 5,000-hp. locomotive, the two locomotives, which measured nearly 182 feet long, were fully independent of one another and capable of operating individually as separate engines.

They were delivered to the Union Pacific at Council Bluffs in April 1939 as Nos. 1 and 2. UP and GE must have had high hopes for these locomotives and they were treated to a full promotional scheme including staged publicity runs for photographers and moviemakers. After initial tests on the UP, the turbines toured the U.S. and were even inspected by President Franklin D. Roosevelt. During May and June they returned to the UP for extensive tests where they operated in a variety of services on several different routes.

Despite the publicity and praise heaped on these pioneering turbines, they had exceptionally short active careers. In June 1939 they were sent back to GE's Erie, Pennsylvania, facility, where they languished before being scrapped in 1942 during World War II.

GAS-TURBINES

Serious interest in gas-turbine technology dated to the turn of the century but was not perfected until the mid-1940s when wartime interest in turbines for aircraft engines spurred considerable research and development. Although GE had expressed interest in building a gas-turbine-electric locomotive in the late 1930s, it did not build one at that time. The first such machine was built in 1941 by Brown Boveri for the Swiss Railways. In the late 1940s, GE decided to further its turbine development toward rail-

In 1954 Union Pacific took delivery of 15 gas-turbines based on an earlier group of 10 such locomotives that had been delivered in 1952. The later group had distinctive open catwalks that earned the units the nickname of "veranda" turbines. The 74 is shown between assignments at Cheyenne in 1957 with a fuel tender, which was an afterthought to these burly locomotives. The turbines didn't lay idle very long, for they consumed almost as much fuel idling as they did while running! *John Dziobko*

Gas-turbine 61 smokes along the Overland Route main line in Wyoming with a meat train that includes a block of stockcars filled with live meat. *Otto C. Perry, Denver Public Library, Western History Department*

road applications and built, with Alco, a double-ended oil-fired turbine electric demonstrator, No. 101. This later became UP No. 50 and performed extensive tests on UP main lines, with an emphasis on the heavily graded and exceptionally busy Cheyenne–Ogden route. This prototype was a rare example of a bi-directional, double-cab, internal-combustion locomotive in the U.S. Almost all diesel-electrics used in North America feature a cab at only one end as was the case with steam locomotives. While straight electric locomotives typically are double-ended, and around the world railways use double-cab diesels, the double-cab configuration was rare in the U.S.

The turbine demonstrator was an enormous 83-foot-long locomotive, riding on eight powered axles in a B-B+B-B configuration. It produced 4,500 hp.—far more power than offered by any single-unit diesel—and was generally an impressive machine, although initially it suffered from a variety of break-in difficulties. Unlike the steam turbine built a decade earlier, this locomotive received the attention and treatment required to solve its performance and reliability concerns. One of its primary difficulties was a decline in tractive effort as its fuel supply was depleted. This was solved by the addition of auxiliary fuel tenders to carry the locomotive fuel.

Union Pacific was sufficiently impressed with the demonstrator and ordered 10 turbine

Assisted by numerous UP and SP EMD diesels, gas-turbine No. 16 drifts downgrade along old U.S. 30 with an eastbound freight near Borie, Wyoming, in July 1965. *Mike Schafer*

locomotives. The first production turbines were delivered in January 1952 and numbered 51 to 60. These were single-ended machines that resembled the prototype and delivered 4,500 hp. The railroad deemed these successful and followed with a second turbine order, Nos. 61 to 75. The members of this group were popularly known as "Veranda Turbines" because of the external catwalks along the sides of the locomotive; the earlier turbines were fully enclosed.

UP's successful turbine fleet led to premature speculation that the gas-turbine might supplant the diesel as the preferred American locomotive type. However, although the gas-turbine proved extraordinarily powerful, its potential application was extremely limited. The locomotive was only efficient when operating at speed with heavy tonnage on the main line. Consequently, it was ineffective in service where it was not producing its greatest potential. Initially this was not a concern for the UP, which only intended to use the locomotives in relatively fast, long-distance, heavy freight service. The turbines were also extraordinarily loud, like a jet engine—a characteristic that earned them the nickname "Big Blows." They were especially unpopular in heavily settled areas and ultimately banned from operating in some Southern California communities because of their excessive noise.

In the late 1950s, UP ordered another fleet of 30 vastly more powerful turbine-electric locomotives from GE. These were six-axle locomotives that produced an astounding 8,500 hp. each, making them the most powerful single-unit locomotives ever constructed. Even the most powerful AC traction diesel-electrics constructed today only produce a maximum 6,000 hp. per unit. In *Motive Power of the Union Pacific*, author William Kratville points out that their enormous output actually depended on the external temperature. Actual output varied considerably from just 7,800 hp. in very cold weather to more than 10,500 hp. in high heat. The locomotives were designed to operate at a maximum of 65 mph and produced a starting tractive effort of 146,000 pounds. In their twilight years, these last turbines were a fixture on UP's Overland Route main line between Omaha and Ogden, though primarily west of Cheyenne.

UP's last turbine was a home-built experimental coal-fired gas-turbine using the hulks from a Great Northern electric and a UP Alco PA diesel cab, No. 80, built in 1959.

A few days after turbine 16 was photographed on the east slope of Sherman Hill (previous page) on July 4, 1969, the photographer has stumbled upon it again, but this time some 480 miles west of Cheyenne at Ogden. It stands ready to take a freight eastward and will leave Ogden yard as soon as the arriving westbound in the foreground clears. *Mike Schafer*

Union Pacific retired its gas-turbine fleet at the onset of the 1970s. What doomed these phenomenally powerful locomotives on UP was not their limited service abilities or extreme noise, but advancements in diesel-electric technology and relatively poor turbine service availability. Initially, one of the great benefits of the gas-turbine was that it burned

Bunker fuel oil, which was much cheaper than diesel fuel. While the turbine had higher fuel consumption than diesels, its overall fuel costs were about the same as diesels. In later years diesel technology improved to allow regular diesel locomotives to use less-expensive fuels, making turbines less advantageous. Also, by the late 1960s, dual-engine, eight-axle diesels were being built that approached the output of UP's turbines, thus eliminating another significant advantage of turbine power. The turbines had a poor availability record—about 80 percent of the time. Even UP's late-era steam fared better than this, and diesels were much better. Kratville indicates that the turbines averaged about 10,000 miles per month.

Index